US-CHINA TECH WAR

US-CHINA TECH WAR

What Chinese Tech History
Reveals About
Future Tech Rivalry

NINA XIANG

Copyright © 2021 by Nina Xiang

All rights reserved. No part of this publication may be reproduced, distributed, or transmitted in any form or by any means, including photocopying, recording, or other electronic or mechanical methods, without the prior written permission of the publisher, except in the case of brief quotations embodied in critical reviews and certain other noncommercial uses permitted by copyright law. For permission requests, write to the publisher; please refer to https://www.ninaxiang.com.

Sold by: Amazon Digital Services LLC
Language: English

First Edition

(Paperback) ISBN: 9798533900034
(eBook) ASIN: B098YSDSD6

Imprint: Independently published

To SARS-CoV-2

Contents

Introduction 11
1. China's Technology DNA 19
   1.1 The Needham Question 20
   1.2 From Jesuits To The Eternal Question 28
2. History of China's Semiconductor Sector 39
   2.1 Pre-1980: Collateral Damage 40
   2.2 Pre-2000: Trial And Error 47
   2.3 Post-2000: New Era, New Challenges 62
3. SMIC 71
   3.1 An Identity Crisis 72
   3.2 Sword of Damocles 93
4. Huawei HiSilicon 107
   4.1 The Success And Curse Of Being Bundled 108
   4.2 The U.S.'s Trump Card 120
5. A War With No Winners 127
References 141

Introduction

The shifting global hegemony and the rise of new superpowers rests upon technology. From the steam engine to the modern transistor, from the Empire on which the sun never sets to America's gunboat diplomacy, the crowning of every powerful nation has been blessed by the magic of technology. Technology drives the wheels of history and the jet engines of the future.

In this current nascent age of 5G and artificial intelligence, technology has become the core driver of economic growth and a key variable of geopolitical competition. As technology seeps ever deeper into our lives and society, it morphs into an embodiment of values, a symbol of national strength, and a stage on which the greatest duel in history is being portrayed.

The contest for global technology supremacy between long-time technology superpower, the United States, and a rising challenger, China, is being played out in the devices we use, the protocols upon which information travels, and the platforms on which we conduct business and play. Moreover, this "technology war" – a somewhat exaggerated but overall fitting term – is often intertwined with and featured prominently in the more comprehensive U.S.-China geopolitical rivalry encompassing economic, military, and ideological battlefields.

Since the Trump administration, a new narrative has gained popularity in describing the dynamic between the two countries: that the U.S. must find ways to compete and push back against China's technological rise, which is based on state capitalism and techno-authoritarianism. Forced technology transfer, intellectual property infringements, government subsidies, aggressive industrial policies, cyber theft, and trade secret theft are how China advanced technologically. All these rule-defying behaviors must be countered with forceful actions to correct them. So goes the portrayal of China's ascension.

No one but former President Donald Trump put this line of thought in more colorful language. The term he coined, "China's economic aggression," has become *de facto* wisdom. "The era of economic surrender is over"; "We can't continue to allow China to rape our country"; "(China has perpetrated) one of the greatest thefts in the history of the world"; "(China is) ripping us left and right"; "(the Chinese *modus operandi* is) lie, cheat & steal in all international dealings"; he claimed.[1]

While most scholars wouldn't go to this extreme (at least publicly), the framework of the debate has been firmly set in this tone. This framework establishes a causal relationship between China's "mercantilist policies" and the outcome of China's technological achievements. It combines "economic aggression" and "unfair trade practices" with "anti-competitive behavior" to generate an across-the-board generalization of China's technological advances. Throw in other buzzwords like the "whole-nation model" and "techno authoritarianism," and the discussion on the U.S.-China tech war often becomes a muddy pool of selection bias and logical leaps.

Chinese Emperor Taizong said during the Tang Dynasty: "With copper as mirror, one can dress properly; with history as mirror, one can understand the rise and decline of history." To better examine how the U.S. and China arrived at the current stage of this competition and how likely this contest will evolve in the future, this book aims to accomplish something that is missing in the current debate: a more comprehensive and deeper analysis of how China's tech sector developed, with an emphasis on China's long history that is daily remembered in China but almost always forgotten by the West.

We will trace the trajectories of China's technological development all the way to ancient China. Then, by carefully combing through the modern development history of major tech industries, we focus on China's semiconductor sector to draw insights from detailed case studies and historical comparisons to understand what is fundamentally driving China's tech advances. Does China want to succeed to best America, or is China's drive today part of a much longer march through history?

It becomes clear then, that at a minimum, to generalize the technological rise of a giant nation like China on behavior patterns is an over-simplification. To concoct one theory about how China's tech developed ignores different sector dynamics: for example, the online e-commerce and semiconductor sectors are hugely different, and their growth trajectories are not the same.

And to view the Chinese government acting as a monolith is wrong too. Not only does each technological sector possess different growth and market characteristics, but scholars have also long cautioned against viewing China's various levels of governments as a whole behaving uniformly. When peeling the Chinese history onion, it quickly becomes overwhelming to attempt to establish one overarching pattern encompassing different sectors across different historical periods.

That is not to say there is nothing to theorize or conclude. For the purpose of engendering a more provocative conversation, this book focuses on fresh angles and new hypotheses that compliment existing commentary and studies. In other words, the book is written to provide an alternative narrative or an opposite perspective to ones that readers are familiar with in the West, as far too often, even pro-China gesticulations from the West are still naively muddied by Western points of view.

For example, we must be cautious contributing all of China's tech success to the so-called whole-nation model. Terms such as state capitalism and mercantilist policies are often used interchangeably to describe how Chinese government planning, industrial policies, state intervention, or manipulation led to China's tech success. But a review of history shows that many of China's tech successes were the result of following market economics, and many of China's tech failures resulted from state capitalism. In the semiconductor industry alone, it is proven again and again that state projects inconsistent with market dynamics are destined to fail. Despite decades of industrial policy, China has failed to achieve Beijing's objective in semiconductors, and China's tech is still dangerously reliant on foreign technology.

This reliance indicates that forced technology transfers haven't worked effectively to narrow China's gap with other leading countries. In fact, the most advanced tech couldn't be forcefully transferred. As South Korean memory chipmaker Hynix Semiconductor CEO, O.C. Kwon, said, "We are not concerned about any possible leakage of technology into Chinese local companies...(Chip making) is not something you can do by stealing other company's technology. For example, in manufacturing processes today, there are close to 500 process steps. From design to mass production takes more than two years based upon IP and know-how from hundreds and thousands of engineers."

Indeed, the greatest technology transfer to China may have taken place via the free flow of Chinese students and engineers who studied and worked in the U.S. and other developed countries, as well as leading technology talents working in China. As Taiwanese chip manufacturing giant Taiwan Semiconductor Manufacturing Company's legal counsel commented about one of its top experts joining rival Samsung: "He just needed to tell Samsung to not go toward a certain direction when Samsung tried to decide its R&D efforts to save Samsung an enormous amount of energy and time."

Other factors such as the open exchanges among scholars, the unhindered flow of investment, and the growth and massive scale of Chinese private corporations' ballooning R&D expenditures all might have contributed more to China's technological progress.

But fundamentally, China's technological development is the result of China being integrated into the global supply chain. It is a two-way choice, in which foreign companies decided to outsource to China, and China accepted to being bundled with Western technology. China's tech sector developed as part of, was based on, and was inseparable from an increasingly globalized supply chain and tech ecosystem.

During the past seventy years, the tornado of migrating global supply chains has swept through other countries and regions – Japan, South Korea, Taiwan – and left those regions transformed into technologically sophisticated nations. There was a time when it appeared that the same pattern would play out in China, but the winds have shifted and even reversed during the past decade.

Looking at history, the U.S. had reacted consistently when its tech supremacy came under attack. In 1987, nine members of the U.S. Congress smashed a small Toshiba radio with sledgehammers at a press conference on Capitol Hill because the Japanese company had violated export control regulations by selling computer-guided multiaxis milling machines to the Soviet Union at an estimated cost of $30 billion in lost American technological superiority.[2] And Japanese cars were smashed by angry American autoworkers for loss of jobs amid accusations of illegal dumping by Japanese firms.

One day after signing the Plaza Accord in 1985 that sharply devalued the U.S. dollar to cut the American trade deficit with Japan, President Reagan said that "When governments permit counterfeiting or copying of American products, it is stealing our future, and it is no longer free trade." An American economist exclaimed, "The way Japan Inc. operates...(is) government and business work hand-in-glove and business moves jointly."

Another political scientist concluded that "...Japan as a closed society, driven by totally selfish economic motives, unfairly exploiting American military protection to dump its industrial-technological products on America while driving Americans out of their jobs."[3] In addition, IBM Corp. alleged that Fujitsu Ltd. copied IBM's mainframe operating-system software. Honeywell said Japan's Minolta stole its patented technology for a camera.

In the case of South Korea, American chip maker Micron Technology, Inc. accused Korean rivals, including Samsung, of selling chips in the U.S. market for less than fair value in 1993 after Korean firms gained market share in America. As a result, Korean semiconductor firms were hit with 10 to 50 percent import tariffs on anti-dumping grounds. Because South Korea didn't pose an all-around threat to U.S. technological supremacy, U.S. actions were narrowly focused on a number of industries such as chips and car batteries.

If these U.S. actions and language seem familiar, it is because the U.S. is implementing the same strategy for countering China's tech rise. But China represents a completely different rival. With a domestic market that could be much larger than the U.S. and enormous international ambition, China has a solid foundation to support a decoupling from the U.S.-led tech system. Decades of integration and talent exchange prepared China to have all the necessary tools to build another tech ecosystem on its own. Equipped with a different ideology and political system, a confident China is unlikely to avoid blatantly challenging the U.S.

We are still at an early stage of this historical tech rivalry. The U.S. has much more ammunition in its arsenal. Besides what it has already done – crippling Huawei and other Chinese companies in their semiconductor supply chain – the U.S. can wreak havoc in many other key Chinese tech sectors such as operating systems, high-end medical equipment, and airplane engines. On the other hand, China holds its own nuclear option: to engineer a total breakout from the U.S. tech system at the cost of hurting both parties.

If policymakers on both sides remain rational and if there won't be any surprises in the economic or military realm, a total decoupling is not in the interest of anyone. The most likely scenario is partial decoupling, with the boundaries of this decoupling constantly shifting with the geopolitical winds. This creates a highly uncertain and unstable operating environment for companies and industries by producing greater market volatility and disruptions. At a personal level, we could all encounter more instances of inconveniences and abnormalities similar to the ones brought about by the COVID-19 pandemic. Life could become more complicated and filled with unpleasant surprises.

This book has five chapters. The first chapter looks at China's technology evolution from ancient times to 1949. The second chapter examines the overall development timeline of China's semiconductor industry from 1949 to the present day. Chapters three and four review the history of two key Chinese semiconductor companies, Semiconductor Manufacturing International Corporation (SMIC) and Huawei's HiSilicon. These two companies represent the pinnacle of China's semiconductor supply chain in chip manufacturing and chip design, respectively. The last chapter offers an analysis of lessons that could be drawn from reviewing China's tech history and how it applies to the analysis of the current U.S.-China tech rivalry.

The book originally planned to cover the histories of all major tech industries in China, including telecommunications, the Internet, electronics, artificial intelligence, and aerospace. But after covering just one sector, semiconductors, it became clear that the original plan was too ambitious. Maybe the other uncovered sectors could be subjects of future books.

I'd like to thank my family and friends for the support they offered me during the writing of this book. The SARS-CoV-2 virus made me appreciate so many things in life that I had taken for granted. The book was contemplated and written during the 18-month stay-at-home conditions. As the book is being finished, a new life attitude is etched in me: to live without fear.

To SARS-CoV-2 virus; to our challenging future; to all who have conquered fear.

1. China's Technology DNA

"Why, between the first century B.C. and the fifteenth century A.D., Chinese civilization was much more efficient than occidental in applying human natural knowledge to practical human needs."[4]

"The essential problem [is] why modern science had not developed in Chinese civilization (or Indian) but only in Europe."[5]

1.1 The Needham Question

Ke Ji is one of those Chinese words that consists of two characters that have contrasting meanings. *Ke* means science, which is defined as "the intellectual and practical activity encompassing the systematic study of the structure and behavior of the physical and natural world through observation and experiment.⁶"

Ji means technology, which is "the application of scientific knowledge for practical purposes, especially in industry" or "machinery and equipment developed from the application of scientific knowledge.⁷"

The Chinese ancestors' belief in *Yin* and *Yang*, the philosophical concept of dualism, helped make such words with contrasting characters prevalent in the Chinese vocabulary. They decorate the Chinese language and are frequently used. Words like *Wei Ji* (crisis/ opportunity), *Duo Shao* (many/few), *Bei Huan* (sadness/happiness), *Shi Fei* (yes/no), *Gui Jian* (superiority/inferiority), *Seng Si* (birth/death), and *Dong Jing* (movement/stillness) are constant reminders of the universe's marvelous contradictions and poetic harmony.

Sometimes, such linguistic features prove to be uncannily prescient. In examining China's technology development history from thousands of years ago up to the past few decades, one central theme is why China was once strong in *Ji* but ultimately did not advance meaningfully in *Ke*. As British historian Joseph Needham famously asked: "Why did modern science, the mathematization of hypotheses about Nature, with all its implications for advanced technology, take its meteoric rise only in the West at the time of Galilio?", and why it "had not developed in Chinese civilization" which in the previous many centuries "was much efficient than occidental in applying" natural knowledge to practical needs?⁸

Before we delve into the topic, it's worth noting that such imbalances between *Ke* and *Ji* still persist to some extent today. Even if China is considered a tech powerhouse today, its strength is undoubtedly in technology application rather than fundamental scientific research.

Today, Needham's Question evolves to another query: Can China truly make strides in science when there is no freedom in speech and ideas? As American sociologist Robert K. Merton proposed, totalitarianism leads to conflict with the traditional assumptions of modern Western science. Authoritarian systems tend to impose a radical ideology and therefore are not conducive to technological innovation.[9] Do these hypotheses still stand in China's case today?

We will discuss this question later. For now, let's keep our gaze on the past and examine what technological and scientific achievements China made in pre-modern days. Beyond the popularly acknowledged "China's Four Great Inventions" of the compass, gunpowder, papermaking, and printing, many other lesser-known early scientific or technological discoveries in China were sometimes far earlier than their contemporaries.

For example, Chinese mathematician and astronomer Zu Chongzhi (429-501 AD) calculated the value of Pi (π) as between 3.1415926 and 3.1415927 during his lifetime. He achieved the result by refining the π algorithm of Chinese mathematician Liu Hui from around the 3rd century. His calculation is a big improvement from Archimedes' (287-212 BC) approximation of the value of π to be greater than 223/71 and less than 22/7. European mathematicians would not surpass Zu's record in accuracy until around 800 years later[10].

Chinese mathematicians also expressed the idea of Gaussian elimination, an algorithm for solving linear equations, around 179 AD, far earlier than German mathematician Carl Friedrich Gauss first published it in 1826[11].

And in looking at the stars, Chinese scholars have made meticulous astronomical observations. As early as 613 BC, Chinese historians recorded the appearance of a comet, and in 28 BC, sunspots were recorded in China, among the earliest records of such astronomical events. Around

185 AD, the appearance of a nova, a transient astronomical event that causes the sudden appearance of a bright "new" star that slowly fades, was recorded in China and was perhaps the earliest historical record of supernovae.

During the Tang Dynasty around 700 AD, astronomer and monk Seng Yixing conducted an ambitious national astronomical survey by taking measurements from the north at Tiele (now southwest of Ulaanbaatar, Mongolia) down to the south in Jiaozhou (now central Vietnam). Based on the measurements of the sun's shadow relative to the distance among different observation points, Seng Yixing was able to calculate a portion of the earth's meridian. It is among the earliest and most accurate efforts to determine the length of the meridian by conducting surveys in ancient times.

The mastery of mechanics and meticulous observations of ancient Chinese astronomers were reflected in creating one device: the Song Dynasty water-powered armillary sphere and celestial globe tower. It is a large-scale automated astronomical instrument invented and manufactured around 1086-1093 AD and regarded as the earliest astronomical clock in the world. It is driven by water power and integrates astronomical observations and timekeeping systems.

Moreover, even though the original equipment was destroyed, a manuscript of how to make the device with 66 illustrations and descriptions of 150 parts survived. In 1958, Chinese researchers began reconstructing the novel device, and the reconstructed clock worked just as it was originally designed.

For architecture, Chinese engineers created long-lasting works such as the Dujiangyan, an ancient irrigation system constructed around 256 BC that is still used today in Sichuan province for irrigation and flood management. The Anji Bridge is an open-spandrel segmental arch bridge built in 605 AD and is the world's oldest bridge of that type made of stone construction.

Generations of Chinese artisans perfected complex mortise and tenon joint structures to build magnificent wooden formations that survived earthquakes and floods. The oldest standing wooden building in the world, the Buddhist temple Horyu-Ji, originally built in 607 AD in Japan, incorporates much of Chinese planning and construction techniques while exhibiting locally suited modifications.[12] The Nanchan Temple, built-in 782 AD, is the oldest surviving wooden architecture that used the same techniques and architectural systems in China. This unique engineering system is still widely used today.

In agriculture, Chinese farmers planted crops in rows as early as the sixth century BC after learning crops would not affect each other if grown this way and would actually accelerate their maturity. Chinese inventors created the planter around the second century BC and greatly improved the efficiency of growing plants[13].

For more leisurely scientific pursuits, Chinese scholar Han Yin (around 200BC-130BC) was the first to recognize that snowflakes have "six points."[14] The first reference in Europe to the uniqueness of snowflakes was in 1555 when Scandinavian bishop Olaus Magnus described snowflakes as an assortment of crescents and arrows.

These are all examples exhibiting the sophistication, meticulousness, and ingenuity of a people that were undoubtedly great original thinkers, inventors, engineers, and astronomers. So it makes Needham's Question particularly relevant. Why had modern science not developed in China?

Some argue the question itself confuses two different concepts. China was always good at *Ji*, or technological applications, but never really good at *Ke*, or scientific research. Therefore, the question is invalid because *Ke* was not China's technology tradition in ancient times. Professor Wu Guosheng at the School of Humanities of Tsinghua University writes:

" He (Needham) often uses the two words 'science' and 'technology' together, which makes people think that he confuses science and technology, making technology interchangeable with science. If he says that ancient

China had technology, or that it was far more advanced than that of the West, that might make sense. But he said that ancient China had science and it was very advanced, which is very confusing."[15]

In other words, technology and science are two different concepts, requiring completely different approaches, logic, and methods. Moreover, one does not necessarily lead to the other. Needham's Question then becomes: "Why was China good at *Ji*, but not so good at *Ke*?"

A cruder way of asking this question is, why could Seng Yixin calculate a portion of the earth's meridian but couldn't take a further step to calculate the whole length of the meridian and perhaps hypothesize the shape of the earth? Why were Chinese astronomers great at making automated astronomical clocks but didn't try to establish a theoretical model of the relative positions of the earth, the sun, and the stars? Why were Chinese engineers able to build irrigation systems lasting millennia but never asked the deeper question of "why" and perhaps take a step towards theorizing about gravity?

These questions are not hard to understand once we understand how China viewed and conducted technology affairs in ancient times. Since Chinese history began, its literal and intellectual class regarded their greatest purpose in life as helping the monarch better manage state affairs and maintain good governance. The Confucian classics have a phrase, "improve oneself, preside over one's family, govern one's states, and bring order to the world," [16] which was the life-long pursuit of Chinese intellectuals for thousands of years.

For the smart, inquiring minds of ancient China, reading classics, abiding traditions, and pursuing a life of fulfillment by governing one's state was recognized as the highest achievement at the personal level. The virtues of the ancient classical era were viewed as the ultimate values that nations and people should emulate. China's history books were filled with cautious tales of those who went against classical virtues and ended up miserable. So, fundamentally challenging established values and authorities, like how Copernicus challenged the existing model of the universe, was not in the Chinese intellectuals' cultural DNA.

Moreover, there were strong and rigid institutional arrangements for China's scientific efforts. Science and technology were part of state affairs like politics, the economy, military, education, agriculture, and diplomacy. From the rulers' perspective, science and technology were viewed only via the lens of managing the state. They were relevant so long as they applied to bettering the economy and people's livelihoods.

And under this framework, a group of officials engaged in science and technology work. Throughout China's history, all science and technology work related to governance was organized and managed by corresponding official institutions, and government officials were appointed to preside over their affairs. For example, during the Tang Dynasty (618–907 AD), arithmetic was one of six scholarship bureaus established by the central government. The state set up separate bureaus to study medicine, calendar calculations, and astronomy. These bureaus were staffed by government officials, who were also moonlighting as mathematicians, astronomers, doctors, or academic researchers at the same time.

They were either appointed by the emperor, recommended by ministers or selected from top performers in the imperial examinations. Higher authorities reviewed and assessed these officials and quasi-scientists periodically to determine their demotion or promotion potential. As a result, the well-known ancient Chinese scientists were mostly government officials, and their achievements were often the outcome of official tasks.

As such, Chinese scientific and technological development was decidedly pragmatic. Areas closely linked to managing state affairs were most advanced. Among them, agriculture, astronomy, arithmetic, and medicine were the most studied areas where China achieved the greatest progress. Exploring the mysteries of nature simply for the sake of discovery was never the starting point for China's scientific and technological efforts.

Because science and technology were studied to help administer governance, there was little need to explore the reasons behind a finding. Thus, generations of Chinese researchers aimed to achieve pragmatic functional improvements and didn't venture to ask the bigger question of "why." Theorizing or hypothesizing about how the world functioned was also not part of ancient Chinese research traditions.

Ultimately, on a philosophical level, the prevalence of Buddhist, Confucian, and Daoist philosophies emphasized nature-human harmony and social order hierarchy. They espoused the concept of "heaven" or "the nature's way" or "*Dao*," which were considered too complex to be comprehended by mere mortals. Humans were to accept such "nature's way" and live accordingly.

For example, in the traditional Chinese cosmology, "heaven" was the supreme existence with a will governing all things on earth. The monarch was the "son of the heaven," acting on behalf of and was restricted by the will of the "heaven." Astrology was studied to get to know the will of the heavens and determine how government affairs should be directed accordingly.

Such thinking tied astronomy with astrology and calendar-making, and this made astronomy a method to serve as a guide for state affairs. The government directly controlled and managed all these efforts, and astronomy took on a sacred and mysterious official function. Making astronomical instruments, establishing astronomical stations, and formulating the promulgation of calendars were symbols of political power. The purpose of studying astronomy in China was not about exploring the laws of the physical world.

Moreover, Chinese theories such as the theory of yin and yang and the theory of the five elements were metaphysical and mystical. These theories were universally applicable to all things in a general and vague manner. Because these theories could be used to explain everything, they hindered – whether consciously or subconsciously - people's scientific pursuits for specific and analytical exploration of the natural world.

So at a personal level, a Chinese intellectual's ultimate objective in life was to serve the state. The purpose of their studies was practical. On an institutional level, science and technology efforts were often government undertakings, focusing on realistic matters, not theories. On a philosophical level, nature was perceived to be too complex to be understood by mere humans, and so nature-human harmony was the ideal pursuit of human existence.

This idea explains the two important characteristics of China's scientific and technological traditions in ancient times: a) They focused on practicality and functionality, not the fundamental reasons behind why something happens; and b) They were tools for governance, and they were not seen as independent pursuits.

The forces of this tradition were so great that, even when technological breakthroughs were made, their power was harnessed to reinforce the existing characteristics. For example, China developed movable type printing as early as the eleventh century, but this didn't lead to the awakening of individuality and a spiritual revolution as Europe saw centuries later. Instead, printing helped solidify conformity in China.

"In China, beginning with the Song, since new technology made printing cheaper, private scholarship and a literate public grew. Collecting and borrowing books became an established custom with some private collections containing over 30,000 volumes. Local schools and academies established libraries, mainly containing printed editions of Confucian classics, histories, literary collections, philosophical works, and some books on Buddhism and Daoism.

With more books available, a passion for reading continued, and during the Ming dynasty, was no longer monopolized only by scholars, but also an increasing literate population. Although the love of books continued to flourish, private scholarship slowly diminished, and academies and libraries were placed under government control and the public no longer had the same access to books it wanted to read. Instead, books the state thought the public should read were printed in order to control ideology and manage its economy and borders after years of Mongol rule. Thus, printing became an instrument of the bureaucracy, strengthening the state and the civil service examination system, and placing Confucian scholar-officials in central leadership roles."[17]

These deep, rigid, and overwhelming traditions lasted for thousands of years until roughly the time of the Industrial Revolution when they were mercilessly smashed to pieces by the arrival of superior Western science and technology.

1.2 From Jesuits To The Eternal Question

The history of the violent clash between China and the West during the 19th century and thereafter are well-written topics. But we will look at this period from the perspective of science and technology with some stories that highlight these dramatic events.

The first story took place centuries before the violent clash of fire and blood. It was during the beginning of the eighth year of the Kangxi Emperor's reign in 1669, on one sunny day at the Meridian Gate in the Forbidden City. The 15-year-old Kangxi Emperor had ordered an official contest in front of the whole imperial court between two calendar-making expert groups. One group was led by Yang Guangxian (1597-1669), a Han government official and then imperial head astronomer; the other was led by Ferdinand Verbiest (1623-1688), a Flemish Jesuit missionary.

Verbiest's senior colleague Johann Adam Schall von Bell (1591-1666), a German Jesuit and an able astronomer, had successfully participated in imperial calendar-making work under earlier Ming Emperor Chongzhen and Qing Emperor Shunzhi. Johann Adam Schall von Bell's calendars provided more accurate predictions of eclipses of the sun and the moon than Chinese ones and were therefore favored by the emperors.

Johann Adam Schall von Bell was appointed as the director of the imperial observatory and the tribunal of mathematics. But his success brewed jealousy from Han officials, and chief among whom was imperial scholar Yang Guangxian, who questioned the Jesuits' theory that the earth is round by asking:

"If really the earth is round, then why wouldn't those who live on the bottom part of the globe fall off? Moreover, water will flow toward lower grounds. If you Western countries are directly opposite to us, which means you live on the bottom part of the earth and water would all flow to you, then how can there be land for you to live there?"[18]

Yang also made public pleas. "We would rather there are no good calendars in China than to have foreigners live in China." After Yang made many accusations against the Jesuits, including their alleged plans to rebel and "ill attempt" to forecast "a short life" for the Qing dynasty, the observatory officials led by Johann Adam Schall von Bell were given death sentences in 1666[19]. Emperor Kangxi was 12 years old and was not yet ruling as an emperor.

So the official contest organized by Emperor Kangxi in 1669, the second year after he took over power to rule, was a moment to test the superiority of two different calendar-making theories. He ordered each group to predict and measure the length of the sun's shadow at noon.

Ferdinand Verbiest used a sundial to measure the precise position and length of the needle's shadow at noon, but an official from Yang's group failed. He was helplessly sweating and made repeated calculation errors. The result spoke for itself, and Emperor Kangxi concluded that the Western calendar-making theories were more accurate. He dismissed Yang's officials and appointed Ferdinand Verbiest to preside over imperial calendar-making.[20]

The event was essentially political maneuvering by Emperor Kangxi to expand his authority and to suppress Han officials in the imperial court, but the symbolic victory underscored the widening gap between China's rigid, stagnant technological development and the West's explosive breakthroughs at that time.

Over a century earlier, Nicolaus Copernicus introduced Heliocentrism, an astronomical model in which the Earth and planets revolve around the Sun at the center of the Universe. This marked the beginning of the Scientific Revolution. The West established and perfected scientific methods in the decades following that, leading to Isaac Newton's publication of *Mathematical Principles of Natural Philosophy* in 1687, which paved the way for the Industrial Revolution.

Emperor Kangxi was the most avid student of Western science. He studied astronomy, physics, chemistry, math, and Western music from foreign missionaries serving in the imperial court. He set up a laboratory in the Forbidden City to concoct medicines and learned how to inoculate with the Smallpox vaccine. After experimenting on his children and court ladies and observing the positive effects, he ordered the vaccine to expand into other parts of the country.

He was also interested in human anatomy, and he personally dissected a hibernating bear. He even experimented with planting hybrid rice in a garden inside the royal palace.[21] But as explained in the previous chapter, Emperor Kangxi wouldn't think to jump outside of the strong Chinese traditions to initiate broad scientific enlightenment in China.

During the Ming and Qing dynasties, many Western missionaries came to China with the goal of introducing Christianity to the Middle Kingdom. The missionaries, the most well-known and the one with the earliest "success" being Matteo Ricci (1552-1610), used gadgets like self-ringing bells, prisms, telescopes, the globe, chronographs, and other advanced scientific knowledge and devices like European maps and astronomy, to knock open the door of China's upper literary class and ultimately gain entrance to the imperial court.

Often risking their lives, the missionaries' goal was to spread Christianity. They frequently ended up having a more visible and prominent effect of spreading Western scientific knowledge throughout China's literary class and the imperial court. Nicholas Trigault, a Jesuit missionary, brought 7,000 books ranging from architecture to mechanics collected from across Europe to China during the early 17th century. His journey from Lisbon, Portugal to China took two years and three months, and only eight out of the 22 people survived the trip.[22]

But no amount of brave missionaries' books and watches, or Chinese emperors who admired European science, could break the hard, cold shell of a dwindling empire. The court officials who wanted to learn from Western science had to placate themselves with the idea that Western science originated from China in order to legitimize their efforts. It would take brutal wars and the violent toppling of thousands of years of monarchic rule to open the flood gate of Western science and technology into China.

The most famous European gifts presented to Chinese emperors were those by Earl McCartney of Lissanore (1737-1806), who headed an Embassy sent by King George III (1738-1820) to Emperor Qianlong (1711-1799) in 1792, hoping to negotiate a preferential commerce treaty with China. McCartney presented some usual gifts, including telescopes, planetariums, chandeliers, locks, and watches, and some unusual gifts like artillery pieces, models of the world's most advanced battleship, steam engines, and the spinning jenny. The aim was to impress the Chinese emperor by showing off the most advanced technology from Europe. The ironic ending is now well-known. When Anglo-French troops invaded Beijing and looted the Old Summer Palace in 1860 at the end of the second Opium War, they discovered that the gifts brought by McCartney 68 years previously – the same weapons that just ravaged the Qing army - had been collecting dust in a royal warehouse and were never opened[23]. What would have happened had the emperor opened, studied, and replicated those devices? Would it have been a more even fight?

This leads to the second story, which occurred after two Opium Wars brought the Qing armies to their knees under the assault of superior Western weaponry. The wars awakened the more vigilant portion of the Chinese population to the realization that their country had been lagging far behind Western powers in science and technology. The notion that China must learn from the West became more acceptable and urgent. The long, gentle period of "Eastward spread of Western culture" represented by missionaries and gift-presenting shifted to a panicked recognition to act promptly. "Learning from the barbarians to develop skills to control barbarians" and "Chinese knowledge as a foundation, Western knowledge as practical tools" became popular ideas for how to deal with the uncomfortable awareness of the West being the proven superior military and technological power. Even "total Westernization" was raised as a path for China to move forward.

In this intellectually confusing time, a group of Chinese technicians tried to build a wooden motor ship on their own with nothing more than some translated books with illustrations of the steam engine. The effort was personally funded by then-Assistant Grand Secretary of the State, Zeng Guofan, and led by Xu Shou and Hua Hengfang, two self-taught technicians who had zero experience building ships or steam engines.

In October 1863, a small wooden ship about nine meters long was let into the water for a test sail. Equipped with a self-made steam engine by Xu Shou and Hua Hengfang, the ship sailed very slowly for just one mile before it came to a halt as the engine failed. The steam boiler couldn't supply steam at a constant and stable rate. But to see that the ship sailed briefly was a big step forward already. After all, just a year ago, Xu Shou and Hua Hengfang had toiled in a lab for three months to produce China's first self-made steam engine by hand with the help of only translated books. That engine was tested for a group of officials but only worked a few moments before sputtering.

This learn-from-the-West theme will be a repeated undertaking over the next 150 years, and to some extent, even today. The backdrop remains the same: a vast technological gap with China lagging far behind. But the process of "learn-from-the-West" is complicated by distrust and China's understandable obsession with self-reliance. In October 1863, compared to Xu Shou and Hua Hengfang's tiny motor ship that sailed just one mile in a river, the British "Lay-Osborn" flotilla, consisting of seven steam cruisers and a supply ship, had just arrived in China one month earlier from England. The Qing government purchased these gunboats to help defeat the Taiping Rebellion. Because China couldn't produce modern ships then, buying from foreign countries seemed the only choice.

But the two sides had a misunderstanding. China wanted the British to surrender command of the ships and serve only as technical advisers. The British falsely assumed that the Chinese government would transmit all orders to the fleet through British diplomat Horatio Nelson Lay, appointed as Inspector General of the flotilla by Qing's Prince Gong. After it arrived in China, the flotilla's commander, Captain Sherard Osborn, refused to take any orders from local Chinese officers, saying, "the notion of a gentleman acting under an Asiatic barbarian is preposterous."[24]

In addition, the distrust of foreign powers was deep among Chinese officials. Having already witnessed what European armies did during the two Opium Wars, voluntarily inviting a British fleet into China didn't seem a wise choice. In the end, the Qing government canceled the purchase and paid a large sum to the British as compensation.

This episode reinforced the need for China to produce ships and other modern weaponry on its own. Xu Shou and Hua Hengfang continued to improve their designs and later built bigger motor ships, but Assistant Grand Secretary of the State Zeng Guofan decided he needed a faster solution. It's unclear how much the failed motor ship test contributed to

Zeng's decision to seek a different approach, but a year after that test, Zeng's colleague Li Hongzhang proposed to the Qing government that "(It's better) to find a foreigner selling machinery of an iron factory around the coast to do inspection and negotiate a price (in person right here), so that (the factory) can begin building and making (tools) immediately," and that it is more convenient and faster compared to "appointing a foreigner to buy machinery from foreign countries" or "to send our representatives to foreign countries to learn the skills."[25]

In 1865, Jiangnan Machinery Manufacture Bureau, the first modern military factory in China, was established in Shanghai at an acquired iron factory previously owned by an American merchant. The Bureau was the biggest enterprise in China's Self-Strengthening Movement, or Westernization Movement, during a period of rapid learning and adoption of Western technology, especially military technology. It made guns, ammunition, ships, and machines for the Qing government with speed as its top priority.

Indeed, buying proved to be faster than building. It took Xu Shou and Hua Hengfang, who Zeng Guofan hired to lead the ship building efforts at the bureau in 1867, one year to produce the first machine-powered warship, measuring around 55 meters long with 392 horsepower and 600 tons of weight capacity[26]. It was a far cry from what the pair produced on their own five years previously. But the ship had a Chinese shell and a foreign core. The internal machinery was old repaired foreign parts, while the Chinese factory only manufactured the steam furnace and the hull. This would become a recurring theme in China's technology development in the following centuries.

The Westernization Movement had limited success for many reasons. The Bureau and other enterprises worked as government entities and were very inefficient. There were few qualifying Chinese workers with formal training. Financial restraints were constant. Most importantly, there was no recognition that greater changes in governance, political systems, mindset, culture, and philosophy were needed to make real progress. This attitude would gradually change in the following decades as the 1911 Revolution toppled China's last imperial dynasty. The New Culture Movement promoted the idea of creating a new Chinese culture based upon Western ideals like democracy and science.

From then on, China entered a stage of thorough reforms and rapid adoption of Western science and technology. The beginning of the twentieth century marked the incubation, birth, and expansion of China's modern scientific and technological development. It was a time when the earliest formally trained scientists, researchers, and technicians emerged in China. Modern research institutions and universities were founded, and private enterprises were created for engineers to make use of their skills.

It was a time when China built its first hydropower station, chemicals factory, steel making electronic furnace, light bulb factory, large scale steam engine, 10,000-ton ships, and self-designed airplane[27]. And this leads to the third and final story in this chapter of how China tried to develop its own airplane manufacturing capabilities during the Republic of China era. This era featured many themes that are similar to ones seen today: Chinese students who went overseas to study advanced technology and brought their skills back home to China; Sino-foreign joint ventures; and China's reliance on foreign products and desire for self-reliance. It is amazing that a century later, China would still be grappling with these same challenges.

China's early history of trying to develop a domestic aerospace industry began not too far behind the world's pioneers. In 1909, just six years after the Wright Brothers first flew their airplane in North Carolina, a Chinese technician, Feng Ru, flew a self-propelled aircraft he built for three-quarters of a mile in Oakland, California.[28] It was the first West Coast flight in the U.S. and the first time a Chinese person had successfully flown an airplane. Feng was born in Guangdong Province in 1883 and came to California when he was 12. Interested in machines since he was a boy, Feng worked at ship-building factories, electricity plants, and machinery plants to learn mechanical skills. Later, Feng returned to China to build the country's first airplane company and participated in the 1911 Revolution. He died in 1912 during a flight demonstration in Guangzhou.

Other early Chinese aerospace pioneers were all trained overseas, including Liu Zuocheng, who studied in Japan and made an airplane in 1911 that crashed during its test flight, and Pan Shizhong, who studied in France and made an airplane in 1914.[29] In 1918, the first Naval Aircraft Engineering Office was set up by the Beiyang Government, all staffed with overseas-trained Chinese technicians. In 1923, Sun Yat-sen ordered the founding of the Guangdong Airplane Manufacturing Plant, headed by Yang Xianyi, who had studied in the U.S.

Together with two American airplane engineers' help, Yang made a reconnaissance aircraft and bomber in just two months based on an existing American aircraft. The bomber, named "Rosamond" after Sun Yat-sen's wife, Rosamond Soong Ching-ling, could quickly be made because it used many American parts. The engine, propeller, radiator, fuel tank, wheels, axle, elastic sleeve, and other parts were all made by Curtiss-Wright Corporation, then the largest aviation company in the United States.[30]

The reliance on foreign products and the desire to make them on China's own was a persistent theme. China couldn't make the core parts like engines and propellers by itself, so it focused on making domestic versions of the simpler parts. Many airplanes were made with wood initially, but they were increasingly made with metals like steel and aluminum.

China couldn't generate quality steel or aluminum, but it was an expert with wood after using it for thousands of years for building furniture, houses, palaces, and pagodas. So, the technicians of the Naval Aircraft Engineering Office used domestic fir, white chestnut, camphor, and white pear wood to manufacture the skeletons of the fuselage, wings, tail, hull, and frame of the aircraft. A Fujian raw lacquer was used to decorate the frames to produce lightweight and waterproof surfaces.[31]

But how to best improve and make the more critical parts domestically was always in the minds of the Chinese engineers and leaders. In 1939, the Institute of Aviation Research was established in Chengdu, tasked to research three areas: equipment, aircraft, and aerodynamics. But for many years, it continued to explore how to use bamboo and other wood to manufacture aircraft despite the global trend to use metal. On the other hand, setting up partnerships with foreign companies seemed a more viable option. In 1935, the China-Italy Aircraft Manufacturing Factory was established. The signing parties of the joint factory were Kong Xiangxi, then Minister of Finance of the National Government in China, and the China Aviation Association, an entity composed of four Italian aviation manufacturing companies.

The Chinese government would provide 25 percent of the investment, with the remaining 75 percent financed by the Italian Bank of Naples, whose amount was to be paid off by China in installments over five years. Located in Nanchang, Jiangxi Province, China would provide the land and other local resources, while Italy would contribute the equipment and parts and half of the personnel. The objective was for the joint factory to produce around 20 percent of aircraft parts locally in the first year after production began, then increasing by 20 percentage points for each year until 100 percent of the aircraft parts were built locally by the fifth year. Then, the Italian employees could pass the baton to the Chinese, who would take over control of the factory.[32]

Similar joint venture arrangements would reappear fifty years later when China opened up and again sought to improve its industries via these types of business relationships. Aside from strong parallels in contract terms, these agreements showed similar ambitions in terms of timelines. The 1935 contract was even more aggressive, wanting to produce all aircraft parts in a mere five years, an almost impossible goal that borders naivety. In the end, the factories took two years to be built and were bombed during the Japanese invasion.

The contract ended during the Second World War as China and Italy fought on opposite sides. The aggressive goal of producing 100 percent aircraft parts remains a distant dream today. In 1943, Chiang Kai-shek, the leader of the Republic of China, visited the country's first aero-engine manufacturing plant. Built in a huge cave in Dading County, Guizhou Province, to evade Japanese bombing, the plant's objective was to produce made-in-China aircraft engines. After the visit, Chiang Kai-shek left a piece of calligraphy artwork to the plant. It was a question: "When can our engines be completely self-made?"[33]

Decades of war and domestic chaos during the mid-1900s made China miss many windows of opportunity to develop its technology sector. It wasn't until the 1980s, when China entered a new era to integrate with the world's economy, that the country started picking up the pieces from years of destruction and stagnation to usher in a new chapter.

2. History of China's Semiconductor Sector

> *"We are not concerned about protecting our IP. Memory is very specialized. It is not something you can do by stealing other company's technology. For example, in manufacturing processes today there are close to 500 process steps. From design to mass production takes more than two years based upon IP and know-how from hundreds and thousands of engineers. To build one decent size fab it takes five billion dollars for business scale. So you can't make such an investment just based upon some technology you are taking away from others. We are not concerned about any possible leakage of technology into Chinese local companies. About half of the DRAM production for Hynix comes from the China plant."*
>
> *- O.C. Kwon, CEO of Hynix Semiconductor*[34]

2.1 Pre-1980: Collateral Damage

In 1947 and 1948, when China was at the end of a decades-long civil war between the Kuomintang-led government and the Communist Party of China, something revolutionary took place on the other side of the Pacific. John Bardeen and Walter Brattain at Bell Laboratories invented the point-contact transistor in 1947, and their colleague William Shockley invented the junction transistor in 1948. The three later won a Nobel Prize in Physics, and their invention gave birth to the modern semiconductors industry and heralded the Information Age.

Some Chinese scientists were among the earliest participants in the semiconductor revolution. In 1949, two young Chinese students arrived at Harvard. One 22-year-old Huang Chang[35], a Tsinghua University graduate, came as a graduate student at Harvard School of Engineering and Applied Sciences.[36] The other was 18-year-old Morris Chang – the founder of Taiwan Semiconductor Manufacturing Company (TSMC), the world's top chip manufacturer half a century later – who after moving around Nanjing, Guangzhou, Hong Kong, Shanghai, and Chongqing with his family during the turbulent years of the Japanese invasion and the civil war, had come to Harvard as a freshman.

After Huang and Chang graduated from their elite institutions – Morris Chang transferred to Massachusetts Institute of Technology (MIT) in his sophomore year – they would both work from 1955 to 1958 at Sylvania Semiconductor, a small semiconductor division of an American company making vacuum tubes and transistors named Sylvania Electric Products. Morris Chang shared an interesting story many years later of how he entered the semiconductors industry. Having studied mechanical engineering at MIT and receiving a master's degree, Chang initially wanted to continue his studies and obtain a Ph.D. at his alma mater, MIT. But two times he tried, and two times he failed. He wasn't able to qualify for MIT's doctoral program. Standing in front of the Ph.D. candidate name lists and not able to find his name both times, Chang felt his "self-esteem and self-confidence were all wiped out."[37]

Now being forced to look for other career paths, Chang applied and received several job offers, with Ford Motor Company being the most prominent potential employer. Sylvania Electric Products, however, offered a salary that was US$1 more than Ford's package. Morris Chang asked Ford to raise his salary and was denied, thus pushing the young and stubborn graduate to join the little-known semiconductor company[38]. These twists of events pushed Chang to the emerging semiconductor sector at a time when it was about to take off and change the world. Tasked to help automate Sylvania Semiconductor's transistor manufacturing production lines because of his mechanical engineering background, Chang, being a smart, diligent, and ambitious young man with big dreams, learned everything he could about semiconductors. He, therefore, honed his early skills in the nascent industry that he would one day revolutionize[39].

Huang Chang had a very different career trajectory. As Morris Chang later joined Texas Instruments, Huang Chang didn't take the same offer from the Texas-based semiconductor company. He decided to return to China to help jumpstart the country's semiconductors sector.[40] In the 1950s, Chinese scientists gathered in Beijing and formed a semiconductors research group inside the Chinese Academy of Sciences (CAS).

They included many educated and trained in the U.S. and U.K. with early pioneers of the industry. Huang Chang left the U.S. in 1958, claiming to go on a world tour because of US travel restrictions placed on talent like him, but he eventually returned to Mainland China via Europe, India, and Hong Kong. After returning to China, Huang soon realized that the research environment in China was a far cry from the U.S., as one Chinese researcher later recalled how he first met Huang Chang:

"As soon as I entered the lab, whose walls were bare, I saw a young man in a white coat squatting next to an electric stove. There was a glass beaker on the stove with a few purple-blue silicon wafers the size of a fingernail. He said: 'This is going to be made into a diode.'"[41]

Such was the early days of the transistor revolution: a researcher would use the most basic tools to try to make what was then an advanced technology. For China, to have U.S.-trained talent like Huang Chang work on semiconductors was the best hope it had. After a hundred years of utilizing the same method to learn from Western tech, the Chinese government understood that human talent was the most effective method of technology transfer.

To build up a local talent pool, several overseas-educated semiconductor experts, including Xie Xide and Huang Kun, began a course in 1956 to teach semiconductors at Peking University. Soon, aside from the China Academy of Sciences, other research institutions were established across China to advance scientific research and cultivate more young talent. Dozens of electronics factories were also created and promoted by the government across the country. In 1956, researchers made China's first working transistor inside CAS,[42] nine years after the first transistor was invented. In 1965, China made its first working integrated circuit, just seven years after Jack Kilby of Texas Instruments successfully demonstrated the world's first working IC.[43]

At the beginning of the world's semiconductor revolution, China wasn't a lagging player, largely due to the contribution of the many returnee scientists like Huang Chang. Because of people like Huang Chang, who had studied in top universities and worked in companies that were at the forefront of this innovation, China was able to follow technological iterations in the U.S. and re-create them in China, at least on a small scale.

China was able to make the first transistor, the first IC, a volume production of transistor radios, the switching tubes and germanium transistor computer, and the MOS (metal–oxide–silicon) integrated circuits mainly by returnee scientists' tireless experiments and the mass galvanization of social resources. Making semiconductors in China without direct foreign support allowed China to achieve other technological breakthroughs, including crafting the country's first electronic computer, computers that powered Chinese armies[44], and systems that allowed the "Two Bombs, One Satellite" program[45] to flourish.

During that time, China was in a stronger position in making semiconductors than South Korea and Taiwan, which had little to speak of in terms of semiconductor capabilities back then.[46] This achievement was even more incredible considering the wider social and geopolitical upheaval of this period.

During the 1950s and 1960s, turbulent events like the Anti-Rightist Campaign, the Great Leap Forward, the Great Chinese Famine, the Sino-Soviet split, and the escalation of the Cold War greatly disrupted the Chinese economy and society. For example, in 1956, the Communist Party of China (CPC) discussed how to treat intellectuals and decided that "most of them (intellectuals) are already part of the working class." It deliberated how to transform "private businesses and handicraftsmen." It talked about how "the bourgeoisie as a class has not yet been eliminated," and the country should continue to "fight for the liberation of Taiwan, complete the socialist transformation, and the final elimination of the exploitation system."[47]

By the end of 1955, the government had nationalized all private businesses and officially established a planned economy. Amid constant political movements and the threat of war, some lasting economic development patterns emerged. Centralized government planning began two years after 1949, founding the People's Republic of China. Modeled on the Soviet's "Five-Year Plan" but localized to suit Chinese conditions, China's first Five-Year Plan was drafted in 1951 and aimed to "lay the preliminary foundation of China's industrialization" from 1953 to 1957.

These policies were extensions of similar industrial policies of nationalized key industries and industrial planning from the Kuomintang government during the 1920s and 1930s.[48]

In 1956, recognizing the importance of technology, China made a "12-Year Technology Plan", its first such long-term plan tailored for a sector. The slogan "March toward science" became a buzzword that year and was cited in newspapers everywhere. To meet the country's leader Mao Zedong's vision for China to "rapidly reach world's advanced levels in several decades in economy and culture," the 12-Year Technology Plan listed dozens of major scientific tasks and hundreds of key problems on which China's best minds would focus.

When the working group tasked to draft this plan took over 600 pages of materials to report to Premier Zhou Enlai, Zhou was overwhelmed by the volume and asked them to only focus on the most urgent areas. The working group then zeroed in on six tech areas that were deemed the most critical and urgent: atomic bombs, missiles, computing technology, semiconductors, automation technology, and radio electronics.[49]

Even though the working group correctly identified semiconductors as one of the most critical and urgent tech sectors on which to make progress, the turbulent domestic environment and rigid planning made China's semiconductors industry enter a period of prolonged stagnation during the global industry's first golden era during the 1960s and 1970s.

As the birthplace of transistors, the U.S. continued to lead with innovations, and the industry was transforming from a speculative emergent industry relying on contracts from the U.S. Department of Defense to a thriving commercial private sector that would soon welcome the age of personal computers. Government purchases of semiconductors in the U.S. dropped from nearly 50 percent around 1960 to around 5 percent in 1973.

The rise of consumer electronics like calculators, digital watches, televisions, Walkman music players, VCRs, and later personal computers led to explosive growth for semiconductors. From 1960 to 1970, the U.S. semiconductors market grew 3.7 times, and it further expanded 5.7 times from 1970 to 1980 and held more than half of the world's market. [50] Starting in the 1960s and 1970s, Japan and South Korea grasped the opportunity to develop their own semiconductors industry and made significant progress. Japan would overtake the U.S. leadership position in semiconductors in the 1980s.

China largely missed this growth opportunity because of domestic political upheavals. The Cultural Revolution from 1966 to 1976 upended the normal functioning of the economy. Semiconductor factories continued to open, and lab experiments continued to produce new technology milestones, but there was no working semiconductors industry. It was more a collective, centrally planned, and rigidly carried out effort to meet mostly military and political objectives.

As China was largely isolated from the international community – the PRC was not admitted into the United Nations until 1971 - there was minimal external support or contact. The Soviet Union was the only support China received externally to develop its industrial and military capabilities in the 1950s, including in computers and semiconductors. In 1956, 15 senior Chinese researchers visited numerous Soviet scientific institutions, universities, and factories to learn from the Soviet's experiences.[51] But Soviet technology was rapidly becoming outdated, and the U.S. was clearly leading the innovation race.

An anecdote during this time shows how disruptive and hopeless this period had been for China's tech development. A senior Chinese leader named Chen Boda recognized and tried to steer China to catch this wave of technological innovation. Chen was an alternate member of the Eighth Politburo, the director of the Political Research Office of the Central Committee of the Communist Party of China, and the vice president of the Chinese Academy of Sciences.

As the leader of CAS and one deeply interested in the world's latest technological trends, Chen tried to convince the leadership, including Mao Zedong, that developing the electronics industry needed to be the center of China's industrialization efforts. In one CAS meeting in the mid-1960s, Chen asked, "Recently, the Japanese proposed to 'make the development of electronic technology as a national plan'; East Germany proposed that the electronic component industry has become 'the center of the entire national economy' and that the electronic industry should be 'developed as one of the leading industrial sectors.' What is Japan's intention here? Is the statement of East Germany correct?"

He also proposed to make a 20-year development plan for the electronics industry and quickly develop China's electronics industry to match other countries.[52] In a 1965 meeting of the Standing Committee of the Politburo, Chen's proposal was discussed, and Deng Xiaoping, then a member of the Politburo before he was denounced and sent to work in a factory, didn't approve of Chen's ideas.

Deng said, "All of us had no experience in developing new technologies such as electronics. China has a large population and a weak (industrial) foundation. It may be inappropriate to focus too much on new technology. It's better to keep things as usual and make things stable."[53] Chen's proposal was shelved indefinitely, and he was denounced several years later amid political infighting. His idea of placing electronics at the center of industrialization was criticized vehemently by the People's Daily newspaper as one of his major mistakes.

Indeed, China didn't have the necessary resources to develop its electronics and semiconductors sectors even if Chen's proposal was accepted. Aside from societal upheavals, there was no functioning market and related industrial supply chain that could provide equipment and materials. There was no such thing as market demand and supply. There wasn't much money to use for investment. The quality of the talent pool was far below that of leading countries in the 1950s because there had been little to no exchanges between China and the rest of the world.

While China remained stagnant in semiconductors, the global chips industry continued to boom. The scale of the global semiconductor market expanded four times from the 1970s to the 1980s,[54] marking the beginning of mass commercialization and scalability of the industry. The technological and market gap in semiconductors between China and other leading countries widened to become a canyon. When China woke up from this nightmarish period, it found itself sitting in the dust of a global semiconductors industry that had raced far ahead.

But starting in the 1970s, the situation shifted. China was admitted to the United Nations in 1971. U.S. President Richard Nixon visited China the next year, which led to the two countries establishing full diplomatic relations in 1979. In 1976, the Cultural Revolution ended. In 1977, Deng Xiaoping was reinstated as the country's leader, and the next year, China began its economic reform.

2.2 Pre-2000: Trial And Error

It's no surprise that the two young men with the same starting point at Harvard in 1949, Morris Chang and Huang Chang, had very different careers and lives afterward. In 1958, they both left their employer, Sylvania Semiconductor. That year, Morris Chang joined Texas Instruments, a rising semiconductor firm that had produced the world's first commercial silicon transistor and made the first transistor radio in 1954. At Texas Instruments, Chang met Jack Kilby, who invented the integrated circuit in 1958. He befriended the most prominent semiconductor pioneers, including Gordon Moore, the co-founder of Intel Corp. and the author of the famous Moore's Law, and Intel's other co-founder Robert Noyce. In a speech in April 2021, the 90-year-old Chang remembered those enchanting early days with an audience in Taiwan:

"The semiconductor circle was very small at that time. Once, I had a meeting with Robert Noyce and Intel's Gordon Moore. Everyone was very gentlemanly (in those days). After the meeting, we all went and drank beer together. At that time, I was only 27 years old. Noyce was 31 years old and Moore was 29 years old. We were all very excited, thinking that we were the chosen ones by the heavens, and we were lucky to join the promising semiconductor field. After our drinks, the three of us returned to our hotel, singing songs the whole way as the snowflakes danced around us."[55]

Chang was inside the inner circles of the industry's elite, worked alongside Nobel Laureates and fathers of the semiconductor industry, and got to know them personally. At the same speech, he shared some more intimate stories of these outstanding individuals.

Jack Kilby and Robert Noyce both invented the integrated circuit almost at the same time. Kilby finished earlier, but the integrated circuit would not have been successfully developed without Noyce's inventions. The two had some disputes, but perhaps because of the gentlemanly era, they finally agreed to settle on the statement that they jointly invented the integrated circuit. Jack Kilby won the Nobel Prize for Physics in 2000 for the invention, but Noyce passed away in 1990 at 63. "But Noyce lived a full life. He had a lot of girlfriends. He often flew planes, went diving, swimming (and enjoyed life),"[56] Chang quipped.

By being at the right place at the right time and with the right amount of ambition, Chang's career took off as well. He rose to become manager of the engineering department at Texas Instruments and eventually became the company's vice president responsible for its worldwide semiconductor business. During Chang's 25 years at Texas Instruments, he finally received his Ph.D. in electrical engineering from Stanford University, an undertaking Chang's employer viewed as an investment in a promising industry leader.

But Chang knew that his career at Texas Instruments had reached its limit, and there wasn't much else he could achieve there. That's when an offer to head Taiwan's Industrial Technology Research Institute, a government-sponsored non-profit tasked to promote industrial and technological development in the island, made an offer to Chang as he searched for other opportunities. Soon after joining the Taiwan organization, Chang recognized something new and exciting to do. He started a company focus on manufacturing chips for those who wanted to outsource this function to third parties.

In the early days of the semiconductor industry's development, one company would do everything, including designing, manufacturing, testing, packaging, and selling the chips. Think of Texas Instrument's electronic calculators. The company designed and made the chips and manufactured and marketed the end product all by itself. These types of companies were called integrated device manufacturers (IDMs).

But gradually, companies realized each of the three steps of making chips had very different characteristics in terms of capital investment intensity, technological barriers, and added value. Starting from the 1960s, companies began outsourcing testing and packaging – the final step of the process with the lowest technological barrier and added value, and less capital intensity than manufacturing - to lower-cost regions including Taiwan, the Philippines, Singapore, Hong Kong, and Japan.

Naturally, the next question was: will chip manufacturing, which required high capital investment with high technological barriers and high added value, be outsourced? There wasn't a consensus back then, but Chang saw it as an inevitable trend for the industry's future.

One interesting encounter led Chang to draw his prescient conclusion. Chang was briefly the chief operating officer of General Instrument Corporation from 1984 to 1985 before joining the Taiwan government-sponsored non-profit. A friend called Chang to ask his company to invest in the semiconductor startup the friend was establishing. The friend said he was looking for a US$50 million investment and promised to send Chang a business plan in two weeks.

But three weeks passed, and no business plan came. Still interested in the startup, Chang called his friend to inquire what happened. The friend apologized and explained that he didn't need US$50 million anymore because his startup would only do chip designing, not chip manufacturing. Therefore, he only needed US$5 million, and he was able to secure the money himself. "That was the first time I heard there was a company only doing chip design. If there were companies focused on chip designing, there must be companies focused on chip manufacturing. One year later, I fulfilled my idea and started founding TSMC," Chang later recalled.[57]

In 1987, a near-retirement-age Chang (aged 56) founded TSMC in Taiwan to specialize in chip manufacturing. Being the pioneer of the pure-play foundry business model, TSMC played a critical role in driving the emergence of the so-called fabless businesses, which referred to companies that focused on chip design and outsourced chip manufacturing to third parties like TSMC.

Fabless firms were light in capital investment with high technological barriers and high added value. Companies such as Apple, Qualcomm, Advanced Micro Devices (AMD), and Nvidia were the resulting successes of the fabless business model. These companies were a stark contrast to IDM firms like Intel and Texas Instruments and helped push up demand for outsourcing chip manufacturing services.

In pushing for this division of labor, TSMC achieved great success itself, inking double-digit growth for decades and becoming the world's largest and most advanced foundry. It had to overcome many challenges. In its first few years, TSMC struggled because its business model was ahead of its time. Chang's old friend Gordon Moore didn't think it was going to work.

But Chang's relationships with industry titans played an important role in ensuring TSMC's success. Intel, whose then CEO was Chang's close contact, Andrew Grove, awarded a contract to TSMC as one of the startup's first clients. Intel's support attracted more clients to TSMC. With Chang at its helm, TSMC steadily rose and dominated chip manufacturing, especially in the most advanced chips decades later.

On the other hand, Huang Chang didn't participate in the global semiconductor industry growth at all. After returning to China in 1958, he started teaching at Peking University in the Physics department. In 1965, he joined a team developing China's aerospace integrated circuit series to support the country's military missiles and launch vehicles. The integrated circuits Huang and his team developed under a challenging environment – the scientists had to manually saw-off silicon wafers and polish them by hand due to the lack of high-precision equipment[58] – were used in China's various types of strategic missiles from the 1960s to the 1980s. Huang's work remained in the military and teaching domain throughout his career.

But elsewhere in China, changes were happening in the 1980s as China opened up to the world. After missing out on the semiconductor's golden development era in the 1960s to 1970s, China woke up to find itself lagging far behind the U.S. and was even behind neighbors Japan and South Korea. In 1977, there were over 600 semiconductor companies in China, but they were all small and technologically backward. The annual production of these factories combined was only around one-tenth of the monthly production volume of a Japanese semiconductor company with 2,000 workers.[59] As China's economic reform began, semiconductors became an important technology sector for the country to focus on once again.

In 1982, China's State Council drafted another development plan for integrated circuits with the aim to close the gap with other nations and gave companies more freedom to function according to market forces. The obvious, easiest, and quickest proven path was to learn from other countries, like Japan and South Korea did before. Many Chinese semiconductor companies began importing foreign technology.

One successful example of this strategy was Jiangnan Radio Equipment Factory, based in Wuxi in Jiangsu province. In 1980, it imported a color and black-and-white TV integrated circuit production line from Japan's Toshiba Corporation. As the two countries' relations warmed, the process was smooth and swift. Over 150 Japanese technicians came to Wuxi to help the set-up and operation of the 5-micron production line. In just several years, the factory increased its production to 30 million units annually and helped power a boom of domestically-made televisions. Made-in-China televisions saw production grow 5.5 times from 1981 to 1985, during a period when many Chinese families bought their first television sets.[60]

But overall, this wave of technology imports during the 1980s was not successful. From 1981 to 1985, a total of 33 Chinese entities imported integrated circuit production lines or equipment. Only a few production lines ended up being successfully operational and achieving volume production of chips.[61]

There were many reasons for the failure, including the lack of central planning. Many projects were duplicating one another, as different local governments attempted to support local companies while not fully coordinating with others. Additionally, some only imported the equipment without importing technical support and process know-how. Some imported outdated production lines, which became obsolete when they were completed. Some lacked subsequent capital or suffered mismanagement. These challenges would be a recurring theme in the following decades.

Recognizing the problems, Beijing took action. In 1986, the central government proposed an upgraded development plan, the Seventh Five-Year Plan for the IC industry. In 1989, it drafted an industry development strategy for 1989 to 1995. Both plans emphasized coordinated efforts focusing on several national-level projects to serve as levers to jumpstart the entire industry.

One of such projects was Project 908, drafted in 1990 with investments of over RMB2 billion (roughly worth around RMB200 billion or US$31 billion today). The major component of the project was investing RMB1.5 billion to build a chip production line with a monthly capacity of 12,000 6-inch wafers with design rules of 0.8 to 1.2 microns.

As a comparison, a TSMC's foundry that started production in the same year had a monthly capacity of 88,000 wafers. While the 6-inch wafer size was comparable to other foundries of the time, the manufacturing processes of 0.8 to 1.2 microns were significantly behind others. For example, a foundry at NXP Semiconductors, an American fab, made 250 nm chips in 1991.[62]

The evolution of semiconductors has been to produce bigger size wafers from 1-inch wafers 30 years ago to 12-inch wafers now, while the process node has decreased from several microns to 5nm at present. It meant the factory, Wuxi Huajing Electronics, would be behind industry leaders significantly when it was completed. But for China, it would be a great leap forward in catching up with global peers, improving China's most advanced manufacturing processes from 2 to 3 microns to 0.8 to 1.2 microns.

But Project 908 turned out to be a disaster. Because Wuxi Huajing was funded by the state, the project required numerous government studies, reviews, and approvals. It took two years to complete financing approvals, three more years to import the production line from Lucent Technologies in the United States, and two more years to build the factory. When the factory was completed seven years later in 1997, the company suffered around RMB240 million loss that year as monthly production was a meager 800 wafers, far smaller than planned.[63]

Moreover, industry leaders kept innovating during the 7-year period, as Moore's Law predicted that the number of transistors in a densely integrated circuit doubles about every two years. In 1996, Japan's NEC produced 16 nm chips, while a foundry of Advanced Micro Devices (AMD) made 50nm chips a year later.[64] The gap between the Wuxi Huajing factory and industry leaders widened even further. The situation was made worse because bank loans financed the factory. This enormous debt burden worsened Wuxi Huajing's finances.

The disastrous outcome of Project 908 demonstrated the weakness of the planned economic development model and the steep learning curve the Chinese government faced moving toward a market economy. Beijing made all the mistakes it could make and learned a costly lesson: the old way of planned national projects wouldn't work in a highly commercial, fast-evolving, market-driven, and technologically challenging global industry.

Lessons learned, the Chinese government wasted no time at a second try. In 1996, Project 909 began aiming to invest RMB4 billion, doubling that of Project 908, to build an 8-inch wafer production line with a manufacturing process of 500 nm. The key entity of Project 909, Shanghai Huahong Microelectronics Co., Ltd., was established that year. The goal was to significantly improve China's industry standing and narrow the technological divide with industry leaders.

A number of changes were made this time. Financing capital was appropriated from the State Council and Shanghai municipal fiscal budget in a 6:4 ratio and was provided immediately. The capital was injected into an independent stock company as capitalization instead of bank loans. All government bureaus and agencies shortened approval time and simplified the review and approval process. The company was directed to function according to market demand and constantly upgrade its product lines to follow market trends closely.

These changes led to improved results. Under a joint venture between Shanghai Huahong and Japan's NEC, the main production line took only 18 months to complete. The next year in 2000, the company made a profit amid a booming global semiconductor market. The line also produced 20,000 wafers monthly, and the manufacturing process was 350 to 240 nm, significantly narrowing the gap with leading firms.[65]

But the success was short-lived and limited. Huahong NEC suffered a loss in 2001 as the global chips market slumped amid the dot-com bust. In addition, it didn't lead to China achieving many technological advances on its own. In other words, not much technology was transferred to the Chinese partner.

Japan's NEC provided the joint venture's technology, staff training, management, and product orders. From China's perspective, the joint venture was akin to an NEC production line operating in China where Shanghai Huahong couldn't translate what it learned to produce self-researched and self-developed products.

The process of technology learning, digestion, trial-and-error, and reinvention by the Chinese partner from the joint venture was challenging, especially when the know-how gap was large. In the end, Shanghai Huahong was able to design and produce very low-end and marginal products like non-contact IC card chips with independent intellectual property rights to be used by the local Shanghai transportation systems. Still, it didn't significantly improve the Chinese semiconductor industry's overall technological level.

The 1980s to 2000s were a period of trial and error for China's semiconductor industry. The government made mistakes and gradually improved how it supported the growth of the domestic chip sector, which remained weak, small, segmented, and technologically backward. In 1994, the output and sales of integrated circuits in China only accounted for 0.3% and 0.2% of the world market share, respectively. Its share of the mainland Chinese market was less than 15%. The prevailing technology was over a decade, or more than three generations, behind the U.S. and Japan.[66]

China's integrated circuit sales grew from RMB110 million in 1981 to RMB7.95 billion (less than US$1 billion using the 1981 exchange rate) in

1999.[67] In contrast, the global semiconductor market was US$169 billion in 1999.[68] China's chip industry achieved some growth, but because of how backward the industry was, the gap with global peers widened.

During the same period, China's electronics industry developed rapidly. Television production grew from 2.5 million in 1980 to 49 million in 1999, expanding nearly 19.6 times.[69] Similar growth was seen in refrigerators, air conditioners, washing machines, and other home appliances.

The personal computers sector, amid a global explosive expansion and the most important electronics product during this period, grew even faster. The average annual growth rate of the added value of China's computer equipment manufacturing industry (35.08%) was faster than the average annual growth rate of the U.S. (17.23%) and other countries. The added value of China's computer industry in 2005 was 408 times that of 1985, and the industry's share of the world's total jumped from 0.5% in 1985 to 46% in 2005.[70]

The incredible growth of China's electronics sector resulted from migrating global supply chains as low-end electronics assembling work was outsourced to low-cost countries like China. It was based on imported chips and imported parts. For the Chinese computer brands that rose to prominence during this time, there were no viable, domestically-made computer chips to use. China was in the midst of implementing Project 908 and Project 909 and trying to set up commercially viable chip manufacturing factories, making chips that were still generations behind international counterparts.

Moreover, the main battleground wasn't computer chips. It was about competing for China's domestic computer market. Previously, domestic computer brands saw their market share plummet from 67 percent in 1989 to 22 percent in 1993, as foreign brands including IBM, AST, and Compaq dominated the Chinese computers market.[71] But at the end of the 1990s, domestic computer brands including Legend (later Lenovo),

Founder, Hisense, and Great Wall had regained dominance, occupying over 60 percent of the Chinese market.

Chinese electronics companies had to move from first mastering low-end tech, then gradually to middle and high-end tech. Liu Chuanzhi, the founder of Lenovo Group, later recalled that computer parts like CPUs, memory, and displays were 85 percent of a computer's cost. "We didn't have the capabilities to develop core technologies like CPUs or operating systems...so we (can only) use mature technologies," he said.[72]

Indeed, it was unrealistic for Chinese companies, still at an early stage in their learning curve, to operate in a market economy and tackle challenging technology problems. China lacked the core elements to succeed in semiconductors during this period. Talent and students didn't want to be in the semiconductors industry because the pay was uncompetitive since very few semiconductor companies could be successful.

The technology China could access was outdated, making technological advances more difficult. The fast-evolving nature of the semiconductor sector –Moore's Law – means it was more challenging for laggards to catch up. All this resulted in China's deepening reliance on foreign chips. The more China assembled refrigerators and computers for exports and domestic consumption, the more chips it bought. China's chip imports ballooned from a very small base in the 1980s to hundreds of billions of U.S. dollars in the early part of 2010. In 2013, China imported US$231 billion chips.[73] In 2019, that figure would grow to over US$300 billion.

It's enlightening to contrast China's semiconductor industry with that of South Korea during this period. Despite both countries eyeing semiconductors as a strategic industry and offered strong government support, they ended up with very different outcomes. Korea's semiconductor sector scored an annual growth rate of 25.5 percent from

1984 to 1992, more than two-and-half times faster than the global semiconductor industry's growth rate (10.6 percent).

From being a marginal destination for low-tech outsourcing in the early 1980s, South Korea became the world's second-leading producer of DRAM (Dynamic Random Access Memory), holding 24.3 percent of the world DRAM market in 1992.[74] Moreover, the country made significant progress in technology. Wafer fabrication was only 8.6 percent of total semiconductor production and 4.5 percent of exports in 1984, but they rose to 42.3 percent and 41.2 percent, respectively, in 1992.[75] The country's semiconductor industry successfully evolved from low-tech assembly to technology-intensive manufacturing, paving the way for its dominance decades later.

What factors led to such different results for these neighboring countries? First, the lead actors were different. China's semiconductor projects were led by political figures, not entrepreneurs or businessmen. Project 909's office director, Xia Zhongrui, was the general manager of Shanghai Huahong Microelectronics, the president of Huahong Group, and was formerly an official in the Shanghai Municipal government.

"I didn't work in semiconductor previously and didn't know much about the industry, so I was learning while doing my job," Xia recalled later.[76] Higher up, the leadership work team for Project 909 was set up by the Ministry of Electronics Industry and the Shanghai government. The top decision-making body of Project 909 was a group of politicians and industry outsiders.

In South Korea, the lead players were the semiconductor companies themselves. They were Korean conglomerates, or chaebols, like Samsung and Hyundai. These successful companies had been operating for decades and already secured a solid business and technology foundation for expanding into semiconductors. Such large, experienced, and diversified private conglomerates were still hard to find in China back then.

Secondly, because the lead actors were different, they functioned in completely different ways. In China, the big national semiconductor projects operated more like political campaigns rather than business endeavors. These projects set very specific and political objectives, with Project 909 aiming to build an 8-inch wafer production line with a manufacturing process of around 500 nm. The ultimate goal was to significantly improve the country's semiconductor industry and narrow the gap with other countries.

The Project's leaders were more concerned about achieving that specific objective and how it would impact their political careers. Naturally, they had very low-risk appetites. The first year when Huahong NEC made a profit, the project was viewed favorably. But suffering a loss the next year, it was suddenly criticized as a failure. The performance review of Project 908 was arbitrary, financial, and short-term, leaving little space for risk-taking and long-term assessment. It also made a follow-up investment difficult to secure politically, thus further diminished their chance for success.

In South Korea, the semiconductor companies, led by shrewd and experienced entrepreneurs and managers, understood the industry's cyclicality and took great risks. In the mid-1980s, Korean semiconductor companies suffered heavy financial losses because the world market suffered a downturn. The products they were producing, 64K DRAM, were also being replaced with 256K DRAM. Korean semiconductor firms continued to invest in facilities, talent, and new product research and development despite these challenges.

When the global semiconductor market recovered a few years later, these companies achieved enormous profits. The same contrarian strategy – investing heavily during industry downturns - worked again in the early 1990s and further cemented Korean companies' positions in the world market. This entrepreneurial spirit and risk-taking would not have been possible in China.

Thirdly, government support was structured differently. In China, the government directly appropriated capital and injected it into a new business entity. Even though improvements were made to give an independently established entity more leeway on daily business decisions and financing changed from bank loans to capitalization, the support from the government was directed at the wrong place in an incorrect way. The financing, incentives, tax benefits, and other resource support all centered around achieving a static objective without considering market dynamics and the holistic industrial development trends.

In contrast, the Korean government provided semiconductor firms with subsidies emphasizing research and development, talent training, financing, marketing, and advanced technology absorption. The government launched a national research and development program to partially underwrite related expenses. The government also served as a mediator encouraging collaborative research and development efforts among different private companies. If the Korean private semiconductor companies were the mountain climbers trying to conquer Mount Everest, then the Korean government served as the Sherpa, sharing the load and pulling the climbers by hand to help them complete their tasks.

In comparison, China's government support didn't focus on research and technology. Because the national semiconductor projects' objectives were set to be specifically on monthly production, wafer size, and manufacturing processes, achieving the objective was more important than how it was achieved. Most energies on the projects were spent on securing foreign equipment, completing factories, and reaching production goals. Absorbing the technology and trying to convert any learned know-how in-house were secondary. Even though Shanghai Huahong attempted to do its own R&D on new products, the focus and investment on this effort were far from enough.

Korean semiconductor companies were relentlessly focused on self-research. The Korean producers were first dependent on technology transfers from American and Japanese firms for the 64K and 256K DRAM. But they invested heavily and consistently in self-research for decades. This allowed them to close the gaps with leading firms and eventually became world-class entities themselves.

In 1983, Samsung developed the 64K DRAM and began mass production four years behind leading firms. But by 1989, it was only six months behind leading firms in the mass production of 4M DRAM. In 1991, Samsung produced 16M DRAM concurrently with Japan. Their production volume also reached that of world-leading firms in the early 1990s.[77]

Finally, the Western technology blockade denied China access to advanced technology and talent. For decades, the US aimed at keeping China at least two generations behind global state-of-the-art semiconductor manufacturing capabilities.[78] It meant China could only import outdated production lines, and it had no access to avant-garde technology. The technology blockade against China will be explained in greater detail in later chapters, but as shown above, even if China had better access to technology, its national semiconductor projects were unlikely to create a competitive private semiconductor industry.

China's talent pool for semiconductors was also very shallow at this point. Because semiconductor talent needs decades of study (usually Ph.D. degrees) and professional work experience to become industry experts – unlike Internet talent that may take a much shorter time - China had a dire talent shortage. The education and training of semiconductor talent had fallen into disarray during the political upheaval the decade before. Moreover, during these two decades, smart students and professionals didn't want to work in semiconductors because of poor career prospects.

But as China's reform and opening up expanded, the number of Chinese students studying and working in leading semiconductor companies around the globe multiplied starting in the 1980s. As the new millennium dawned, they would return to China to launch semiconductor startups that became Chinese industry leaders. The age of global integration and great knowledge transfer began, but the road forward was filled with unexpected turns and new challenges.

2.3 Post-2000: New Era, New Challenges

Before China's Communist Party took control of the mainland in 1949, many Chinese Nationalist Party members fled the country. In 1948, TSMC's founder Morris Chang's family took a boat from Shanghai and sailed to Hong Kong. Around the same time as Chang's family departure, another newborn baby took a similar seafaring trip to a different destination. Richard Chang (no relation to Morris Chang) and his parents sailed from Nanjing to Taiwan.

Half a century later, Richard Chang would establish Semiconductor Manufacturing International Corporation (SMIC) in Shanghai, hoping to compete with Taiwan's TSMC. The two men would be locked in a brutal commercial battle that changed the course of China's semiconductor industry.

Their elite parents – Morris Chang's father was in banking while Richard Chang's father was the country's leading steel-making expert – could never have imagined how their young sons would influence strategic power shifts at the national level when they sailed the turbulent waters of the East China Sea. But their fates would meet, and their threaded interactions would get more dramatic and – using Morris Chang's word – ungentlemanly.

For China's semiconductor industry, the beginning of the new millennium marked the end of big national semiconductor projects such as Project 908 and Project 909. It signaled the start of a new era: the emergence of private semiconductor companies founded by talent who had been trained overseas.

Around 2000, as the world was relieved that the Y2K bug did not wreak so much havoc, numerous semiconductor startups were being established in Mainland China by returnee talent. Deng Zhonghan, a University of California at Berkeley Ph.D. and former IBM researcher, established fabless chip firm Vimcro Corporation in Beijing. In 2001, Chen Datong, who studied at the University of Illinois and Stanford University, co-founded a mobile phone chipset company, Spreadtrum Communications, Inc. In 2001, Dai Weimin, a Ph.D. from the University of California at Berkeley, founded VeriSilicon Holdings Co., Ltd., a custom silicon service and semiconductor IP licensing firm. In 2000, Richard Chang, a 20-year veteran of Texas Instruments, founded SMIC, a foundry with the same business model as TSMC, providing chip manufacturing services to chip design firms. Some of these companies later grew to become China's industry leaders.

In terms of government policy, Beijing adopted new methods to promote and support the sector. In 2000 and 2011, it issued two policy documents to encourage the development of the software industry and the integrated circuit industry.[79]

The thinking was more in tune with what other countries did during this period: providing support for private companies to compete and succeed in the marketplace. The specific policy guidelines experienced tweaks later on, but the overall framework remained the same. Notably, starting from the Eleventh Five-Year Plan (2006-2010), Beijing changed the wording of its "Five-Year Plan" to "Five-Year Guidelines," emphasizing the important role of market mechanisms in the allocation of resources.

Specifically, the two semiconductor industrial policies included expanding financing channels and listing opportunities for the targeted industries, tax incentives, research and development funding, preferential administrative treatment such as government procurement and fast-track approval, and incentives for talent education and training.

There were several noteworthy items in the industrial policies during this period. The policies provided more incentives to the software industry than to the IC industry, particularly in 2000. The majority of the 2000 policy document addressed preferential policies for software companies, while policies for the IC sector were not nearly as comprehensive.

For example, the policy proposed creating a special fund to support high-level software researchers to study overseas and hire foreign software experts to teach in China. Software exports could also enjoy preferential interest rates from China's Export-Import Bank of China and state export insurance. There was no such support for the IC sector.

Even for the IC sector, policies focused more on chip design and less so on chip manufacturing. Chip design firms were categorized as software companies and therefore could enjoy the more comprehensive policy incentives offered to software companies. Not only did chip manufacturing companies have fewer incentives, but they also had to compete with subsidized foreign-manufactured chips.

The 2000 industrial policy offered import tax incentives for imported chips manufactured by foreign foundries but designed by domestic fabless firms when such chips couldn't be manufactured by domestic firms. This policy made the decision for domestic fabless firms to outsource their chip manufacturing work to foreign foundries easy and further stretched the gap between domestic and international foundries.

After China issued the 2000 policy, the U.S. raised concerns to the World Trade Organization in 2004 that China's partial refund of valued-added tax on domestically produced ICs would be akin to subjecting imported ICs to higher taxes. A few months later, China decided to amend or revoke the measures and eliminate the availability of value-added tax refunds to local ICs. It represented a period when the U.S. and China could resolve disputes via an international trade body.[80]

Overall, these government policies effectively attracted foreign companies to invest in China, nurturing a group of local private firms. As China became the world's factory for electronics, it made sense for companies to bet on China's rising demand for semiconductors. These led to a boom in the Chinese semiconductor industry.

China's semiconductor industry market size soared from 56.16 billion Yuan in 2002 to 281.43 billion Yuan in 2011, with an average annual growth rate of 19.61 percent, which is much higher than the world's growth rate of 8.75 percent during the same period.

China's semiconductor industry also became more important globally, with its proportion of the global market share rising from 4.81 percent in 2002 to 14.5 percent in 2011. In terms of demand, China became the biggest consumer for semiconductors. The country's semiconductor market reached 923.88 billion Yuan in 2011, up from 229.92 billion Yuan in 2002.

In addition, the Chinese industry became more balanced among chip design, chip manufacturing, testing, and packaging. In 2002, testing and packaging, which had low value-add and low technological barriers for entry, accounted for 80 percent of China's semiconductor industry. In 2011, the three categories were roughly evenly distributed, with chip design and chip manufacturing taking 30 and 31 percent of the industry, respectively.[81]

Chinese companies made progress on technology too. The country's integrated circuit production lines grew from 18 in 2002 to 66 in 2011, with wafer size upgraded to 12 inches from 8 inches. Manufacturing processes improved from 180 nm in 2002 to 90nm in volume production, 65nm in initial production, and 55nm being taped out in 2011. Chip design companies grew from 367 firms in 2002 to 534 firms in 2011, with 41 companies designing 90nm chips.[82]

But as business boomed, the industry was facing persistent challenges. The statistics listed above included foreign companies' operations in

China; therefore, they didn't accurately reflect the capabilities of the domestic Chinese industry.

The biggest and most technologically advanced semiconductor companies were foreign or joint ventures, such as SMIC and TSMC's plants in Shanghai. During the Ninth Five-Year Plan (1996-2000), foreign investment accounted for half of China's accumulative investment total in the integrated circuit sector.[83] It showed how China's semiconductor industry was dominated by foreign players, particularly in high-end products like CPUs. The growth of China's semiconductor industry was, in essence, the migration of global semiconductor firms reallocating some of their production facilities to Mainland China.

Moreover, the reliance on foreign chips deepened. From 2002 to 2011, China's trade deficit of semiconductor products increased from 24.78 billion US dollars to 121.47 billion US dollars, an average annual growth rate of 19.32%.

The integrated circuit trade deficit reached 137.63 billion US dollars in 2011, an average annual growth rate of 22.97% from 2002. Understandably, a great portion of such chip imports were used for assembling mobile phones and computers for export and were not consumed locally.

Looking at China's local integrated circuit production as a share of China's local integrated circuit market, the ratio was also low at around 10 percent in 2010.[84] China could only produce a very small portion of the chips needed for its own consumption, exposing a critical vulnerability in a highly important industrial sector.

Another vulnerability persisted. The global supply chain migration was built on the premise that China's semiconductor industry continued to be decoupled from its electronics industry. China became the largest producer globally for many more electronics products, but these industries continued to be deeply bundled with foreign chip supply chains from the beginning until the present.

Therefore, it was challenging for Chinese semiconductor companies, already inferior in technology and capability, to squeeze into the supply chain. Because the semiconductor firms couldn't become part of the supply chain, they lacked the experience, expertise, and scale required for technology upgrades. Such a cycle was hard to break and kept Chinese semiconductor companies further behind their peers. In other words, the prosperity of China's electronics industry and the stagnation of its domestic semiconductor sector were two sides of the same coin.

Lastly, despite government industrial policies and support, little progress was made toward self-reliance on chip manufacturing capabilities. This lack of progress would become a great puzzle to solve years later. Still, during the first decade of the new millennium, it simply didn't make any commercial sense for Chinese companies to enter the chip manufacturing business.

The ruthless pursuit of smaller gate sizes, larger wafer sizes, and scale meant companies needed to increase investment by about 20 percent per year in leading-edge technology nodes.[85] Only a handful of companies, including Intel, Samsung, and TSMC, could keep up the pace. The characteristics of the industry were winner-take-all, and laggards would fall ever further behind.

Take Huawei as an example. After Huawei's access to advanced chip manufacturing capabilities at foundries like TSMC was cut off in 2020, many people wondered why Huawei hadn't started chip manufacturing when it began to design its own chips many years ago.

A look at Huawei and TSMC's operating numbers in 2010 showed it was simply unrealistic for Huawei to get into chip manufacturing. In 2010, Huawei made 23.8 billion Yuan (US$3.6 billion) net profit on revenues of 185.2 billion Yuan (US$28 billion).[86]

TSMC, meanwhile, generated a net income of US$5.13 billion on consolidated revenue of US$13.32 billion. Huawei made more revenue but had a much lower profit margin, 12.8 percent vs. TSMC's 38.5 percent.

That year, TSMC's regular R&D budget was US$940 million, and its capital expenditures were US$5.94 billion, [87] nearly double that of Huawei's net profit. Not considering the lack of technological expertise, Huawei's business scale was insufficient to support the intensity of capital and R&D investment for chip manufacturing.

If the financial calculus of entering the chip manufacturing business was unrealistic for Huawei, one of China's most successful technology companies, the numbers would have been far less viable for other Chinese companies.

This period was also marked by the Chinese government's prevailing wisdom to fully commit to the fabless model, which was rapidly gaining converts and appeared to be the industry's future.

From 2005 to 2010, the compound annual growth rate for foundries (chip manufacturing) and fabless (chip design) were 9 percent and 11 percent, respectively, much higher than the global industry's average growth rate of 4 percent.[88]

If the industry's specialization between chip design and manufacturing was to deepen and China continued to lack chip manufacturing capabilities, buying chips or outsourcing chip manufacturing was the obvious decision.

As a result, China's chip design companies made significant progress. From 2001 to 2011, China's integrated circuit design industry grew 52.3 percent annually, much higher than the world IC design sector's growth of 12.8 percent.

It was also 28.1 percent higher than China's overall IC industry growth rate during the same period.[89] Some of the Chinese fabless companies grew to become world-leading firms, including Huawei's HiSilicon and Spreadtrum Communications: both were among the top 25 integrated circuit design companies globally in 2011.

On the other hand, chip manufacturing didn't grow nearly as rapidly. Chip design's ratio of the industry increased from 7 percent in 2001 to 36 percent in 2011, but chip manufacturing's ratio grew only slightly from 22 percent in 2001 to 27 percent in 2011.

The most telling fact was that Beijing didn't invest in chip manufacturing plants from 2000 to 2009.[90] It signaled to the industry that the focus on chip manufacturing from the highest level of government was not strong

In addition, the geopolitical situation during the time appeared stable and amicable. The American government even loosened export control schemes on China to allow Chinese companies to import more high-tech equipment. The world was mesmerized by the utopian illusion of globalization and a flat earth. For China to rely on foreign chip manufacturing was the natural evolution of globalized supply chain and industrial specialization. After all, we had come to the end of history. Or, had we?

3. SMIC

"Let me tell you something: High-end semiconductor manufacturing is black magic. Both the processes and tools used for it are very complex. ASML's EUV lithography machine is probably the most complex tool humankind ever developed since it stopped jumping between trees. It took billions of Euros and decades of experience to perfect it. Other experienced lithography machine suppliers failed at it. China has no experience in high-end semiconductor manufacturing tools with the exception of one-off/few-off prototypes."

- Bora Taş on Quora[91]

"It became clear to Moore that, no matter how much science went into conceiving of silicon wafers, there would always be an artlike skill associated with their production."

- Robert Curley[92]

3.1 An Identity Crisis

It is a coincidence that the founder of SMIC, Richard Chang, shares the same family name as Morris Chang, TSMC's founder. And though the two men are unrelated, they share much more than just their surnames. They shared the same tumultuous boat journey from Mainland China to Taiwan around 1948. They both worked at Texas Instruments for a long time: Morris Chang for 25 years and Richard Chang for 20 years. Being 17 years younger, Richard Chang aspired to change the face of the global semiconductor industry, as Morris Chang did before him.

After a long tenure at Texas Instruments and having worked on several semiconductor projects, Richard Chang looked at the world map and realized that at the turn of the millennium, there was only one place he could fulfill his ambition: Mainland China.

It was a time when the trend within the industry of adopting the foundry and fabless models was deepening. Qualcomm and Nvidia overtook Xilinx and Altera to become the top two largest fabless firms in the world in 2001.[93] TSMC became the first Taiwanese company to list on the New York Stock Exchange in 1997[94] and was quickly winning more clients around the globe. China, emerging as a large semiconductor consumer, was virgin turf for advanced chip manufacturing capabilities.

Richard Chang, like Morris Chang, had extensive experience in semiconductor manufacturing. After two decades at Texas Instruments and perhaps feeling the same "bamboo ceiling" as Morris Chang did many years earlier, Richard Chang moved his sights to Asia, where greater opportunities awaited him.

He oversaw the setup and operations of many semiconductor projects in Taiwan, Singapore, Japan, and Mainland China. In 1999, Richard Chang joined a Chinese semiconductor company to lead its efforts in developing 0.5-micron chip production facilities. This Chinese semiconductor company was called Wuxi Huajing Shanghua Semiconductor Co., Ltd.

Huajing, as mentioned in previous chapters, was the company created during China's Project 908 in the 1990s. Because of administrative approval delays and massive debt load (the company's capital came from bank loans), Huajing suffered losses during the first year when it finally achieved production years later. To survive, the struggling Huajing had to lease some of its equipment to a Hong Kong company established by a Taiwanese semiconductor industry veteran, Chen Zhengyu, who was also looking for business opportunities in the Mainland.

Huajing also changed its business model from being an IDM (integrated device maker) to focusing on pure foundry, manufacturing chips for third-party fabless firms, and becoming China's first foundry.[95] After that, Huajing and Chen Zhengyu established a joint venture, Wuxi Huajing Shanghua, to operate a 6-inch MOS (metal-oxide-semiconductor) foundry.

Chen invited his friend, Richard Chang, to the joint venture in Wuxi to help lead opening a new 0.5-micron chip production line. With these market-oriented moves and two Taiwanese industry veterans at the helm, Huajing Shanghua finally generated a profit and became the biggest 6-inch chip manufacturing company in Mainland China in 2004.[96] That year, it was also listed on the Hong Kong Stock Exchange. A failed government project was therefore reincarnated as a successful private company.

Richard Chang didn't stay at Huajing Shanghua for long and had to return to Taiwan. According to one account, the Taiwanese government pressured Chang to return as cross-strait relations worsened in the late 1990s.[97]

Richard Chang soon joined another project in Taiwan called Worldwide Semiconductor Manufacturing Corp (WSMC).[98] Under the leadership of experienced managers and experts like Richard Chang, it began volume production and made a profit in 2000.

At that time, TSMC was engaged in fierce competition with rival United Microelectronics Corporation (UMC) in Taiwan. The two companies did what businesses often do when faced with an emergent fast-growing new rival. They competed to buy out WSMC. Eventually, TSMC won the bidding war and bought WSMC for $5 billion.

In many Chinese media reports, Richard Chang was described as not knowing anything about the TSMC acquisition until it was a done deal. Therefore, long-lasting hatred was planted in 2000 between Richard Chang and Morris Chang, which led to their tough legal fights many years later.

But in one interview, Richard Chang clarified that he was fully aware of the acquisition, participated in the negotiations, and supported the deal.[99] He also suggested that Morris Chang let him go to Mainland China to set up operations there after the acquisition, but Morris Chang did not respond. So an impatient Richard Chang decided to do it alone. He brought a team of hundreds of semiconductor talent from Taiwan and internationally to Shanghai. In 2000, SMIC was born.

Did Richard Chang and Morris Chang have soured relations? Were the ensuing legal battles the result of a personal vendetta? The personal machinations of the two men are perhaps not so important, and a psychoanalysis of what went wrong is not necessary. But the day when SMIC was established, TSMC was mindful of a new potentially dangerous competitor, similar to its previous alertness to WSMC. It is best to look at the events from the perspective of competition at the corporate level rather than focus on personal drama.

The ensuing rapid development of SMIC proved that Morris Chang had every reason to be extremely concerned. Richard Chang had the most important resource: talent. The hundreds of Taiwanese and international top industry talent was the biggest asset for the new company.

The capital was plenty too. From being incorporated in April 2000 in the Cayman Islands to when its American Depository Shares (ADS) were listed in New York in 2004, SMIC raised a total of $1.7 billion from various Chinese and international investors.[100] To ensure SMIC remained independent and international, Richard Chang pooled international investors, including Goldman Sachs, Walden International, Vertex Holdings, and Chinese investors such as Shanghai Industrial Holdings, Beida Jade Bird, together as SMIC's earliest financial investors.[101]

In addition, the company was able to buy the necessary equipment it needed for its plants. In its filing to the New York Stock Exchange in 2004, SMIC disclosed that "To date, however, we have not experienced any major difficulties or delays in sourcing, purchasing, and installing the equipment we need to fabricate wafers for our customers." The company did warn investors that it could be restricted to buying equipment and materials if export controls under the Wassenaar Arrangement or U.S. export control regulations change.[102]

With talent, capital, and all the right resources, SMIC moved quickly. Four months after its incorporation in the Cayman Islands, it started constructing its first fabrication plant in the Zhangjiang High-Tech Park in Shanghai in August 2000. Thirteen months later, it had completed the construction and commenced pilot production; this was an incredible speed for fab plants to launch. In 2002, SMIC began setting up a 12-inch fab in Beijing, which would be China's first once completed, and it acquired a wafer plant in Tianjin from Motorola a year later.

By 2004, SMIC had the largest 8-inch wafer fabrication capacity in China and China's most advanced process technology, capable of 0.18 micron and 0.13-micron process technology.[103] It reached a monthly fabrication capacity of 81,000 wafers in mid-2004 and reached 152,000 wafers monthly capacity at the end of 2005.[104] By one estimate, SMIC became one of the world's top three foundries in 2005, and it contributed half of China's foundry business.[105] By every measure, the performance and growth speed of SMIC was incredible and incomparable to state-led projects like Project 908.

However, for TSMC's Morris Chang, the most important thing was that SMIC was taking existing clients or potential clients away from TSMC. SMIC tried to position itself as an international company with operations in Mainland China. Most of its clients were international IDMs or fabless companies.

In its IPO prospectus, SMIC listed Fujitsu, Infineon, Samsung, Texas Instruments, Broadcom, and Marvell Semiconductors as its customers. These were the target clients for TSMC too. In 2005, SMIC had 254 customers, and its revenues came from clients from North America (40.8%), Europe (27%), the Asia Pacific excluding Japan (26.8%), and Japan (5.3%).[106]

The proportion of Mainland Chinese clients were so small that it wasn't listed separately. China had very few IDMs or fabless firms capable of designing the type of industry-leading chips that SMIC manufactured. But the more important reason was the logic behind SMIC's establishment in China. As explained in its IPO prospectus, SMIC was set up in Mainland China because of the migration of global manufacturing and supply chains.

China was becoming a center of electronics products manufacturing. It saved money for everyone involved to produce the chips in China, where they would be assembled into final products for export. In other words, SMIC was an international firm providing international fabless companies cheaper manufacturing capabilities closer to these chips' final destinations. Its establishment paralleled a global industry trend of moving portions of the global supply chains to Asia in the pursuit of better economics for those at the top of the value chain.

Even though SMIC was still small compared to TSMC, which had $7.65 billion in revenues in 2004, the threat it posed to TSMC was real and urgent. Different from WSMC, an outright acquisition was not an option this time as SMIC's operations were in Mainland China and intertwined with a close Shanghai government partnership. Richard Chang was also determined that SMIC would make its mark on the industry under his leadership.

Morris Chang understood better than anyone else that SMIC, with its talent, capital, resources, and ideal market positioning in the fast-growing Mainland China market, could seriously threaten TSMC's dominant market position given time. So he acted promptly.

TSMC first sued SMIC in 2002 in Taiwan and won an injunction prohibiting SMIC from hiring senior TSMC managers. Because the ruling had no effect outside of Taiwan and therefore couldn't impact SMIC's operations in Mainland China, TSMC then filed another suit in the U.S. District Court of Northern California, alleging SMIC of patent infringement and trade secret misappropriation. TSMC sought immediate injunctive relief against further use of its technology and damages.[107]

In the lawsuit, TSMC claimed that SMIC had hired more than 140 of its personnel, including some key technology staff such as its director of R&D and the manager of quality and reliability. SMIC's vice president of operations, Marco Mora, was alleged to have sent an email to then-TSMC quality control program manager Katy Liu asking for "detailed process flows…including process target and equipment type" for specific logic nodes including the then-advanced 0.18-micron logic nodes.

Mora also asked for TSMC training materials used for staff training. In addition, TSMC claimed that SMIC stole certain patents from TSMC to fabricate an 0.18-micron chip for Broadcom Corp. TSMC believed that the chip could not have been fabricated without using TSMC's proprietary process steps.[108]

The Taiwanese government also put pressure on SMIC and Richard Chang. In 2000, the Taiwanese government determined that Richard Chang "illegally" invested in Mainland China by establishing SMIC, a high-tech enterprise under strict regulation in Taiwan. In 2004, the Taiwanese government planned to fine Richard Chang and sought other punishment, including jail time. In 2005, Richard Chang was first fined 5 million New Taiwan dollars ($155,000) and then 10 million New Taiwan dollars ($310,000).

Richard Chang refused to pay the fine and applied to give up his Taiwan residence. He had been a U.S. citizen for many years. But Taiwan didn't accept his application. Moreover, since the establishment of SMIC, Richard Chang had not gone back to Taiwan for fear of getting arrested until after he exited from SMIC.[109]

In 2005, TSMC and SMIC reached a confidential settlement. SMIC would pay TSMC $175 million in installments over six years. The two parties would cross-license to each other's patent portfolio through December 2010. The settlement also dismissed all pending legal actions without prejudice between the two companies in U.S. District Court, California State Superior Court, the U.S. International Trade Commission[110], and Taiwan District Court.

"With this settlement, we have amicably resolved all of our pending litigation with SMIC and believe that it is in the best interests of our shareholders," the then-deputy CEO of TSMC said after the settlement.[111]

The legal troubles didn't slow SMIC. The company was able to complete a global initial public offering in March 2004, including an offering in the U.S. and Hong Kong, raising $1.8 billion to finance its ambitious expansion plans.[112]

SMIC's four 8-inch wafer foundries in its headquarters in Shanghai, a 12-inch fab in Beijing, and a fab in Tianjin were producing 152,000 wafers a month at the end of 2005. SMIC's joint venture with United Test and Assembly Center Ltd. (UTAC) in Chengdu, a testing and packing plant, also began production. SMIC also planned to expand its foundries in Beijing, Tianjin, and Shanghai and build a new 12-inch fab in Shanghai.

It also signed a contract to manage and operate fabs in Chengdu and Wuhan.

Moreover, SMIC was making progress technologically. It was China's first fab to achieve 90nm nodes manufacturing in 2005. It reached industry-leading yield rates in just nine months in the production of DDR2 DRAM. A team of engineers was developing 65nm and more advanced nodes.[113] In comparison, TSMC was the first foundry to begin 65nm risk production in 2005 and passed product certification the following year.[114] SMIC was catching up with TSMC very quickly, and the technological gap was narrowing.

More importantly, the effect SMIC had on China's overall semiconductor sector was enormous. Being in Mainland China, SMIC positioned itself as a partner of local semiconductor companies. Slowly, more domestic companies began working with SMIC. In 2005, SMIC added 55 new customers from Mainland China. At the end of the year, over 8 percent of SMIC's revenue came from Mainland firms.[115]

The expectation was that as SMIC progressed to master industry-leading manufacturing nodes, it would also help improve domestic chip design firms' technological sophistication. Together, they could advance concurrently to industry-leading levels and migrate a bigger portion of the global chip design and chip manufacturing capabilities to within Chinese borders.

That was exactly SMIC's aspiration. In its 2005 annual report, it noted that after growing at a compound annual growth rate of 33 percent since 2000, China consumed $40.8 billion ICs in 2005, becoming the world's largest regional IC market for the first time.

By 2010, China's IC market was forecast to triple to reach $124 billion. Yet, the gap between China's local demand for ICs and domestic supply continued to widen. Chinese local manufacturers met less than 5 percent of the country's IC demand in 2005.[116] In the age of increasingly globalized supply chains, it made sense for China to close that gap, and SMIC would be the company leading that effort.

SMIC was already the world's third-largest foundry in 2005, and it took around half of China's foundry market that year. It was an eye-popping performance. Based on the potential growth in the Chinese semiconductor market, SMIC could eclipse TSMC if such a trend continued.

In August 2006, TSMC sued SMIC again for breaking the terms of their 2005 settlement agreement. TSMC accused SMIC of "massive corporate espionage" and claimed that SMIC "lavishly copied the information it stole from TSMC, "word for word...and even typographical error for typographical error."

TSMC also alleged SMIC incorporated TSMC trade secrets in the manufacturing of SMIC's 0.13 micron or smaller products.[117] TSMC sought over $1 billion in damages and asked the judge to permanently bar SMIC from selling the contested products in the U.S.[118]

SMIC filed a countersuit the following month, seeking damages for TSMC's "breach of contract and breach of implied covenant of good faith and fair dealing." In its counterclaim, SMIC described "how TSMC, rather than compete in the market place, has undertaken a concerted effort since the previous lawsuits to discredit SMIC by making unfair and misleading accusations."

SMIC said it had complied with the settlement agreement, and TSMC did not voice any complaints for over 17 months, until July 2006 "after SMIC succeeded in meeting a number of major business and technical milestones during Q2 2006."

SMIC claims that "TSMC used the lawsuit and subsequent campaign to repeat its previous campaign to disrupt SMIC's business and valued relationships with its customers."

In hindsight, the most critical variable in this nasty legal fight was SMIC's civil lawsuit against TSMC in a Beijing court. In November 2016,

Beijing Higher People's Court accepted SMIC's suit against TSMC for unfair competition and commercial slander. The action was viewed as SMIC's attempt to involve Chinese courts and to have Chinese courts place "important influence" in a politically sensitive dispute. [119] Considering SMIC's strategic importance to China's semiconductor sector, Chinese courts could tilt the balance.

In January 2007, TSMC requested the California court prohibit the Chinese lawsuit. It then claimed to the Beijing court that the Beijing court didn't have jurisdiction for this case. The California court dismissed TSMC's motion, and TSMC's appeal was dismissed too by an appeals court in the U.S.[120] In July 2007, the Beijing court decided that it did have jurisdiction. TSMC appealed to the Supreme People's Court in China, and in May 2008, the Supreme People's Court upheld the original verdict.

The Chinese court didn't support TSMC's claim that the Beijing lawsuit would amount to repeated lawsuits after U.S. courts had already accepted the case. The Beijing court said that according to Chinese law, when one party sues in a foreign court while the other party sues in a Chinese court, the Chinese court shall have jurisdiction. Even though there were no specific legal standards in Chinese law matching this case's specific situation, the court determined that it had jurisdiction.

Of particular interest in the Chinese court verdict was that the Beijing court determined that this lawsuit was a foreign party-related civil case because SMIC was a foreign legal entity. The Beijing court viewed TSMC as "not foreign" because China's stance has always been that Taiwan is an inseparable part of China. But because SMIC was a foreign entity, the relevant laws of foreign party-related civil dispute applied to the case.

Ultimately, the Beijing court did not provide any additional leverage to SMIC or influence the legal disputes in any significant way. It didn't support any of SMIC's claims against TSMC.

It found that SMIC lacked evidence to support its accusation that TSMC abused its litigation rights and violated the principle of good faith.

It found that SMIC didn't have enough evidence to support the claim that TSMC fabricated and spread false facts to damage SMIC's commercial reputation. It determined that the media reports were fair coverage of the lawsuits, and TSMC didn't intentionally spread false information to the public. It didn't support SMIC's request for a public apology from TSMC and for TSMC to compensate for economic loss.[121]

SMIC's lawsuit in the Beijing court might be a weak case, but the Beijing court showed that it ruled fairly and purely based on the law in this very important case. It wasn't swayed by the implications its verdict would have on a strategically critical industry for China. It appeared that it didn't receive any political pressure from the authorities to act in a certain way. If the timing had been seven years later when the U.S.-China relations began to strain, the Chinese court might have acted differently.

The lawsuits were progressing unfavorably for SMIC. The Beijing court didn't support its allegations against TSMC, and a jury in the U.S. found in favor of TSMC on 61 of 65 trade secret claims after the liability phase of the trial.[122]

In November 2009, the two companies reached a settlement to resolve all pending lawsuits. SMIC would pay TSMC $200 million in cash, as well as stock and warrants that could allow TSMC to take up to a 10 percent stake in SMIC. But TSMC's stake would be passive, and the Taiwanese company couldn't vote for members of SMIC's board of directors. The deal allowed SMIC to continue to use TSMC's trade secrets and technology disputed in the case.

At the same time, Richard Chang announced his resignation from his CEO role at SMIC. Even though Richard Chang told reporters that his resignation was not part of the settlement, insiders believed that his resignation resulted from pressure from TSMC.[123] A 61-year-old and downbeat Richard Chang left the company that he founded and nurtured for nine years, planting the seed of an even bigger crisis for the company.

It was a big win for TSMC. Morris Chang said that he was very happy about the outcome. The monetary compensation was insignificant to TSMC, but it was roughly about a quarter of SMIC's market capitalization then. Partly due to the extended lawsuits lasting for six years, SMIC's Hong Kong-listed shares had dropped around 76 percent from its IPO in 2004 to the time of the settlement in 2009. Since 2008, SMIC dropped out of the world's top three biggest foundries to land at fifth place.

The lawsuits between SMIC and TSMC showed that the global legal system provided adequate legal protection for technology companies. Even though the legal system is not always the most important determining factor in company disputes – as we will see soon in the example of TSMC vs. Samsung– it often worked as intended.

For SMIC, the resignation of Richard Chang was most significant. As a founder, he ensured control and stable operations of SMIC for nine years. His departure left a power void and exposed a fundamental flaw in SMIC's corporate governance: the lack of a controlling shareholder.

When SMIC was established, Richard Chang purposefully pooled international, Mainland Chinese, and Taiwanese capital and resources. As he saw it, SMIC must be an international company to succeed. An international identity would allow the importing of Western equipment and technology to face fewer constraints. It could also leverage the resources and strength of each party to create a more powerful corporation.

For observers, this arrangement made it hard to know what was SMIC's "citizenship." One international media outlet quipped about SMIC: "Registered in the Cayman Islands, the company has its headquarters in Shanghai; its chairman and CEO is Taiwanese; the majority of its investment (he thinks) comes from America; its biggest shareholder is Chinese, and it is listed in both America and Hong Kong. But the main point is that to China, it is Chinese, and to Taiwan, it is simply menacing."[124]

No shareholder held more than 15 percent of SMIC's shares, and no single party dominated the board in its early years. Senior management heralded by Richard Chang controlled the actual day-to-day management of the company. But perhaps it was clear to some observers that China would want to take SMIC into its own hands sooner or later.

But for as long as Richard Chang was the company's leader, he was able to maintain a delicate balance among SMIC's three interest groups: Mainland Chinese capital that wanted to nurture the domestic semiconductor industry; Taiwanese senior management that hoped to make SMIC a dominant international player; and international investors who prioritized a great financial return.

Right after Richard Chang's departure, SMIC seemed able to maintain stability. Jiang Shangzhou, an intimate partner of Richard Chang, took over the chairman's role. Jiang was deputy director of the Shanghai Municipal Economic Commission at the time of SMIC's founding. He was instrumental in planning SMIC and Shanghai's partnership to have SMIC be headquartered in Shanghai.

Jiang was expected to continue playing the role of balancing the interests of all sides, and he shared Richard Chang's belief that SMIC must remain independent and international in order to succeed. He acutely understood that SMIC couldn't compete in the marketplace had it become a semi-state-owned enterprise.

In terms of senior management, David N.K. Wang, a Taiwanese semiconductor executive with prior experience at Applied Materials Inc. and Shanghai Huahong (Group) Co., Ltd., became the new CEO. He represented the interests of SMIC's numerous Taiwanese employees, who had been holding core senior positions within SMIC since day one.

Yang Shining, a Mainland Chinese executive with U.S. citizenship who worked at SMIC during its early years, became a chief operating officer. Yang was viewed to represent the interests of Mainland Chinese staffers and capital. The Mainland Chinese forces had gradually grown their influence but had been ranked second to the Taiwanese groups in the company's hierarchy.

This delicate balance began to crumple in 2008 when SMIC received an investment from a Chinese state-owned telecommunications firm, Datang Telecom Technology. Due to the impact of the Global Financial Crisis, the global semiconductor sector experienced the first year-on-year drop in global dales in 2008.[125] SMIC's loss expanded over ten times to $377 million in 2008 from the previous year.[126] SMIC needed to raise fresh capital urgently.

The semiconductor manufacturing business has very high capital expenditures. It costs as much as over $1 billion or even more to build a foundry. Because SMIC was expanding, sometimes building multiple foundries simultaneously, its capital expenditure remained high.

As a new company, its equipment depreciation and amortization costs were also very high. Other competitors who had been in the business for a long time would have lowered such costs. This is one reason why catching up in the semiconductor manufacturing business is extremely hard. Because of these hurdles, SMIC suffered losses from 2005 to 2009 with expanding negative income.

SMIC's choice of a new investor was limited. Some international private equity giants were interested, but they were not the type of long-term, passive, and patient capital SMIC desired. Existing investors were not interested in putting in more capital because of the repeated losses SMIC was incurring. International strategic investors were out of the question because SMIC needed to maintain independence.

In the end, only several state-owned Chinese enterprises remained on the list. China Electronics Corporation, a state-owned telecom equipment firm, was taken out of consideration for its involvement with the Chinese military. China Resources Holdings reportedly was in the bidding but didn't stay until the end. Datang, the only bidder remaining, sealed the deal.[127]

The transaction was not ideal for SMIC on many levels. Struck at the height of the Global Financial Crisis, the share purchase price was SMIC's historical low point. Datang bought 3.7 billion newly issued shares of SMIC for $171.8 million, taking a 16.6 percent stake of SMIC after dilution. The price equated to 0.36 Hong Kong dollars per share.[128] Just six months previous, SMIC shares were trading at around 5 Hong Kong dollars.

Moreover, Datang invested as a strategic investor, not a financial investor. As a telecom equipment maker, Datang was a customer of SMIC. But it wanted to maximize its own strategic interests by seeking more control, potentially damaging SMIC's long-term stability and prosperity. From the beginning, Datang showed strong interest in taking more control of SMIC. As part of the transaction, Datang appointed two directors on SMIC's seven-person board, and it, therefore, became the most powerful force on the board.

Why was Datang interested in taking more control of SMIC? Industry watchers speculated that Datang was aggressively developing 4G technologies, and it wanted SMIC to support such efforts and build a more comprehensive supply chain for its telecommunications business.

Another speculation was that Datang hoped to improve its status within the central government-owned-enterprises cohort. It was a time when Beijing was pushing for integration among such entities with aggressive goals to reduce the total number of these entities. If Datang could become the owner of China's largest chip manufacturing company, it would be more likely to maintain independence, and its executives could retain their power.[129]

Chairman Jiang understood the danger Datang presented. To balance Datang, Jiang reportedly pushed for China's sovereign wealth fund, China Investment Corp. (CIC), to take a stake in SMIC. Jiang hoped that CIC could become the largest shareholder, but Datang vehemently opposed the plan.[130]

In the end, all parties agreed in 2011 for CIC to invest $250 million in SMIC in exchange for an 11.6 percent stake, and it became the second-largest shareholder behind Datang. Concurrently, Datang injected another $102 million to avoid its stake being diluted and increased its stake to 19.34 percent.[131]

After these deals, Chinese state-owned capital became the most powerful group among SMIC's shareholders. New shareholders Datang and CIC, together with existing shareholder Shanghai Industrial Investment, held nearly 40 percent of SMIC in 2011. The next biggest shareholder group was TSMC, which had 9.54 percent.

Despite the Chinese state-owned capital's increasing weight within SMIC, with independent-minded and neutrally-positioned Jiang as chairman, SMIC maintained a highly delicate balance for a while. But the balance was broken in June 2011 when Jiang passed away from a long-term illness. Jiang had cancer for over a decade but still took on the chairman role because SMIC was in great need of a leader after Richard Chang's departure. His passing ignited a violent storm as different forces within SMIC now openly fought for control.

What ensued was a classic boardroom drama. First, Datang conducted an ambush during SMIC's shareholder meeting in June 2011 and voted against CEO David Wang to continue his directorship. As was the norm among companies in China, only a small amount of investors with over 30 percent of SMIC's shares attended the annual meeting. But Datang held nearly 20 percent of SMIC, meaning its "no" vote alone could end David Wang's directorship. Thus, SMIC lost its only executive director on its board.

Then Datang attempted to make David Wang resign from his CEO role and then have COO Yang Shining take over the helm. Because Datang's two directors on SMIC's board were non-executive directors, they couldn't get involved with the company's daily operation. Datang had formed an alliance with Yang Shining, who grew up in Mainland China, to have him serve as executive director and hoped to make him Datang's agent on the board.

To achieve this goal, Datang offered David Wang three years of his annual salary as compensation if he resigned. Wang rejected the offer. To take away Wang's CEO role required a board vote, according to SMIC's governance protocols. An emergency board meeting was held three days after the shareholders' meeting. Datang only had two directors on the board, and most directors voted to retain David Wang as CEO. A new executive director, the former chairman of Huahong Group, Zhang Wenyi, was elected as temporary executive director.

But the fight for control intensified internally as the Mainland Chinese and Taiwanese forces within SMIC tried to oust the other side. Staffers argued with each other on the internal online bulletin board system. It got so nasty and emotional that SMIC had to close down the online forum. A disgruntled employee shared with reporters an internal auditing file that showed COO Yang Shining evaded a large amount of personal income tax through questionable reimbursement of invoices.[132] This placed SMIC into the swirl of another controversy and negative media headlines.

In the end, the ugly battle ended with a bloodbath for SMIC's senior management. CEO David Wang and COO Yang Shining both resigned from the company in the summer of 2011. It was a lose-lose situation for all parties.

The company experienced a very unstable time with share prices plummeting. Aside from the loss of senior management, many technology talents left or were poached by competitors. The company's operations were significantly disrupted during this time, and morale sank.

The divided board finally agreed on a new CEO, Taiwan-born semiconductor veteran Qiu Ciyun. Qiu was educated in the U.S. and worked at Bell Lab and TSMC in his early career. He was among the hundreds of talent who followed Richard Chang to SMIC from TSMC at the time of SMIC's founding.

Because of different ideas on how to develop SMIC, Qiu left SMIC in 2005. Richard Chang wanted the aggressive expansion to elevate the Mainland Chinese industry, while Qiu believed steady and gradual expansion was more prudent. Qiu then worked at Huahong NEC alongside David Wang, SMIC's CEO, who just resigned. Qiu was also an old friend of Zhang Wenyi, SMIC's temporary executive director.

Qiu's appointment stabilized the Taiwanese forces within SMIC and stopped the talent departures. It also led SMIC in the opposite direction in terms of its development strategy.

Richard Chang's strategy was aggressive expansion and focused on rapidly closing technology gaps. The rationale was convincing. At its birth, SMIC served dual purposes. It was a profit-seeking commercial entity, but the unspoken objective was also to help elevate the Chinese semiconductor industry.

As a commercial entity, SMIC needed to scale up rapidly to finance high capital investment and research costs. The industry's nature meant only foundries with scale could compete, especially for advanced manufacturing nodes. So to elevate the Chinese semiconductor sector, SMIC also aimed to become the biggest company and pursue the most advanced technology. The strategy resulted in repeated losses for many years and a declining share price.

Qiu, who left SMIC many years previous for precisely this difference, could now implement his strategy of stability and profitability. Qiu's slogan was "Let go of ambitions, slow down, and move steadily."

Under this new strategy, SMIC no longer focused on pursuing the most advanced manufacturing technology and instead focused on mature technology. It stopped aggressive expansion and tried to improve the yield rate and maximize the utility rate in its existing foundries. It also sought to focus more on the Chinese domestic market and grow its domestic customer base. "We will prioritize profitability…and invest in advanced technology and capacity expansion cautiously," the company said in its 2012 annual report.

Under this new strategy, SMIC experienced a period of steadily rising financial performance. The company's revenues doubled from 2012 to 2017, the year when Qiu left SMIC. These six years saw consistent profit-making by the company, the longest stretch of profitability it ever had.[133]

The company's market capitalization tripled. In fact, Qiu was the only CEO during whose leadership SMIC experienced share price increases. At the same time, the company's revenue came more from Mainland Chinese companies (including Hong Kong), whose ratio of SMIC's total revenue grew from 34 percent in 2012 to 47 percent in 2017.[134]

But SMIC's superior financial performance came with a cost. The company stopped spending aggressively on research. Its R&D expenditure growth rate shrank during this time.[135] Because SMIC was a late-comer trying to catch up, it always had a much higher R&D-to-revenue ratio compared to rivals such as TSMC.

In SMIC's first eight years, its R&D spending accounted for around 30 to 40 percent of TSMC's expenditure despite SMIC's revenues being only a fraction of TSMC's. However, during Qiu's reign, this ratio fell to under 20 percent, with four of those years falling under 10 percent.[136]

SMIC's capacity expansion slowed to a steady pace. Its pursuit of the most advanced technology continued but was no longer the top priority. In 2012, SMIC saw its 45/40 nm manufacturing node entering volume production. It was also developing 28 nm technology. TSMC, in comparison, achieved mass production of 40nm process technology in 2008 and began providing 28 nm technology in 2011.

This gap widened in 2017. That year, SMIC was trying to improve the yield of its 28nm technology and still developing 14 nm technology. TSMC, however, already achieved 7nm process technology in 2016.

SMIC's technology divide expanded from roughly one generation to two generations behind TSMC.[137]

In hindsight, this five-year period was a rare and precious window for SMIC to expand capacity and catch up with TSMC in scale, R&D, and technology. The U.S.-China relationship was relatively stable. Washington's attitude toward Beijing hadn't shifted 180 degrees yet. SMIC's access to advanced equipment like lithography machines appeared to be decent. But this was exactly the time when SMIC focused on financial performance instead of closing the technology gap.

A deeper look reveals that these chance events may share common fundamental drivers. The turbulent history of SMIC, including its management earthquakes and strategy shifts, is rooted in the company's complicated and vague identity.

To keep the company "independent" and "international" to evade Western technology restrictions, SMIC pooled capital from both Chinese and foreign sources. With its core management and talent team being Taiwanese, SMIC became the perfect battleground where conflicting sects of interest groups fought for control. This amounts to building a tall building with a shaky foundation.

The dual-purpose aspect of SMIC adds additional pressure to the organization. It needed to pursue profits as a private enterprise and serve as a pioneer to elevate China's semiconductor industry. These two conflicting goals were impossible to achieve at the same time. This dilemma led to SMIC's big strategic shifts in 2012 and 2017. In the end, it didn't succeed in fully achieving either objective.

A comparison between SMIC and TSMC provides more insights into how the two companies had very different outcomes. Both companies received government capital and international private capital at their founding. Both received significant government support in the form of financing, tax benefits, land, and other incentives. Both developed under similar government industrial policy to boost local industry. Both sought growth in accordance with the wider global industrial migration trend of their time.

TSMC benefited from the deepening of the foundry/fabless model and global semiconductor capacity migrating to South Korea and Taiwan at the turn of the millennium, while SMIC sought to be a core player in the expected global semiconductor capacity migration to Mainland China in the 21st century.

The first difference was that TSMC had stable leadership under Morris Chang. This afforded TSMC a consistent and clear strategic direction for decades, allowing it to focus on R&D investment and eventually build a deep technology moat. SMIC, however, suffered serious management disruption because of the reasons described above.

TSMC served as a key player in starting and popularizing the fabless/foundry model. It was a trailblazer. The costs of building foundries in the late 1980s and 1990s were also much less prohibitive. SMIC was a late-comer trying to catch up. It faced a much steeper mountain to climb. Aside from exponentially higher costs, it had to tread carefully not to breach the comprehensive intellectual property library of those who came before it.

Also, the supportive policies of Mainland China to SMIC were not as effective and adequate as Taiwan's. The Industrial Technology Research Institute (ITRI) in Taiwan set up the "IC Demonstration Project" around 1980 and poured government support into several select potential industry leaders, including TSMC. In addition, ITRI played a key role in helping to educate and train talent for the industry. Many Taiwanese semiconductor companies and founders came from ITRI.[138]

However, the support policies of Mainland China didn't focus on nurturing just a few potential industry leaders. The China National Integrated Circuit Industry Investment Fund, for example, invested in dozens of companies in a way that the industry calls "sprinkling black peppers all over the pot." This method may make sense for the investment fund but didn't offer enough comprehensive support for potential industry winners.

Moreover, there was no similar organization to ITRI in Mainland China to provide critical research and talent training support. Under the backdrop of a Western technology blockade against China, having a government-sponsored research center may have been counter-productive. Such research would be better conducted by private Chinese enterprises without government ties in order to have better access to Western technology.

Semiconductors, after all, are a dual-use technology deemed by the U.S. that could potentially help the Chinese military. But even for the U.S. government, defining dual-use and limiting dual-use tech access to China was never a black and white matter.

3.2 Sword of Damocles

The technology blockade against China has gone through different stages and didn't become an urgent priority for the U.S. until recent years. After World War II and during the Cold War, the U.S. was primarily concerned with the rise of the Soviet Union. Therefore, its export control regime was about restricting the ability of the Soviet Union to acquire key items that would aid its military development.

The Coordinating Committee for the Control of Multinational Trade (CoCom) was established in 1949 and led by the U.S. to control the flow of three types of goods: conventional arms, nuclear-related items, and dual-use items.

As its name suggests, Dual-use items refer to those that could be used for both military and civilian purposes. Integrated circuits, software, computers, electronics, telecommunications, and information security systems all fall within this category. Understandably, implementing export control of dual-use items would be the most tricky and controversial among the three types of goods.

Before the mid-1990s, American exporters attempted to liberalize export controls, which they deemed as placing them at a disadvantage to foreign competitors as the compliance burden fell on the American exporters. Uneven enforcement among CoCom members meant U.S. exporters might be losing potential markets to countries with less strict enforcement.[139] The delicate balancing act between weighing commercial interests against national security concerns began during the early days of the export control scheme.

The end of the Cold War and the dissolution of the Soviet Union led to CoCom being disbanded in 1994. It was replaced two years later with the establishment of the Wassenaar Arrangement on Export Controls for Conventional Arms and Dual-Use Goods and Technologies (Wassenaar Arrangement), a multilateral export control regime with voluntary members. Its members had expanded over the years from 33 at the time of its founding to 42 countries as of now, including the most technologically advanced countries with the U.S. at its helm.[140]

The Wassenaar Arrangement was a weaker and looser control scheme that only required members to notify each other of transfers of controlled exports. Unlike the CoCom, members couldn't veto other member's exports, and pre-shipment notification was not required under this new regime. The Wassenaar Arrangement was described by some as a "chat society with no teeth."[141]

The Wassenaar Arrangement reflected the wider political climate and American domestic politics at the time. The collapse of the Berlin Wall prompted questions like whether it was "the end of history."[142] Neoliberalism was the prevailing thought of the day, and people marveled at the prospect that "the world is flat."[143] Globalization was believed to spread the magic power of the market worldwide to benefit people in the East and West.

The Clinton administration believed dual-use controls "interfere...with our companies' ability to succeed internationally". It believed that "to control dual-use technologies in the post-Cold War era would be futile" and that "export promotion was the way to bolster America's industries in the increasingly globalized economy."[144]

So despite declarations from the opposition that "American's national security...was being sacrificed at the altar of commerce,"[145] the Clinton years saw a systematic easing of dual-use export controls. Unfortunately for China's semiconductor industry, this period was during the industry's infancy in terms of commercialization and marked by misguided state-sponsored projects.

The 9/11 terrorist attacks in 2001 made the U.S. tighten export control systems. In the case of China, the U.S. resumed a much more delicate balancing dance trying to equilibrate both commercial interests and national security. After all, China, with its 1.3 billion people, was deemed the next super engine charging the global economy.

This balancing act was reflected by the Bush administration's stance to promote "China's peaceful economic development" and encourage Beijing to be a "responsible stakeholder" on the one hand, while at the same time "prudently hedge against...[China's] rapid military buildup."

Export controls, the administration stated, would facilitate hundreds of millions of dollars of civilian high-technology trade annually while denying the export or transfer of any goods that would make a direct and significant contribution to China's military.[146]

In this context, the U.S. implemented the so-called "China Rule" in 2007, a carrot-and-stick policy designed to achieve the above-stated dual objectives. The China Rule imposed tighter restrictions on technologies knowingly intended for military end-use in China while at the same time setting up a "Validated End-User" program to allow trade with pre-approved civilian end-users in China.

Shanghai Huahong NEC Electronics Co., Ltd., a joint venture between Japan's NEC and China's Huahong Group (an entity connected to Project 909), was among the first of five companies approved as "Validated End-User" (VEU) under the China Rule in 2007.[147]

Within the U.S., the debate about export controls of dual-use goods never stopped. When the China Rule was announced, critics were quick to point out that it would negatively impact American business interests in China and do little to slow China's military modernization. Worse, it could even undermine U.S. national security if China turned to foreign competitors.[148] Others pointed out that "the defense industry has grown civilianized" and "dual use has become the rule and not the exception." It was in the interests of the U.S. to "have the Chinese military use U.S. commercial satellites than it would be if China developed its own military alternative."[149]

A government policy review found that "U. S. policies and practices to control the export of semiconductor technology to China are unclear and inconsistent, leading to uncertainty among U. S. industry officials about the rationale for some licensing decisions. Under the Export Administration Regulations pertaining to China, the general licensing policy is to approve applications, except those items that would directly and significantly contribute to specific areas of China's military. We found that the United States approves most licenses for exports of semiconductor manufacturing equipment and materials to China."[150]

Despite the heated debate, the Bush and the Obama administrations largely kept to the "hedging" strategy. The average annual additions to sanctions lists by the two administrations stood at 435 and 533, respectively. But the tide turned dramatically during the Trump administration, with the annual additions to sanctions list nearly doubling to 1027.5, with China taking up the top billings of the sanctions.[151]

Of course, the increasing number of sanctions against Chinese entities under the Trump administration was just a small part of a comprehensive reset of the U.S.-China relationship to "correct" trade imbalances, secure American telecommunication networks, and protect intellectual property, in the administration's own words.

For SMIC, the changing environment was alarming. The most significant warning signal was perhaps the five-year probe by U.S. authorities into Chinese telecommunications firm ZTE Corp. for violating U.S. sanctions on Iran.

The probe ended in March 2017 with ZTE agreeing to pay a massive fine and plead guilty to sanction violations and obstructing justice.[152] But it was the threat that ZTE could potentially lose its abilities to import U.S. goods, including processors – and therefore unable to continue operations - that made the situation clear to the Chinese business community: any of them could face sanctions and lose the abilities to purchase U.S. parts critical for their operations. There was a Sword of Damocles hanging above each of them.

This provided an urgent and real impetus for the Chinese semiconductor industry to sandbag domestic alternative solutions as no government policies did before. Decades of industrial policies didn't make the industry significantly less reliant on foreign suppliers and parts.

SMIC's development history showed that its growth was based on global supply chain integration and migration. Even though SMIC was viewed as the main actor to elevate the Chinese semiconductor industry, especially in chip manufacturing, its supply chains were almost completely reliant on foreign suppliers, which provided key equipment like lithography machines and chemicals. Not to mention for a great portion of its history, it served mainly as a China-based manufacturing facility helping foreign chip design firms to produce their chips in China used for local assembling then destined for export.

Indeed, a review of China's policies in semiconductors shows that the industry missed its objectives again and again. For example, the 12th Five-Year Plan on National Strategic Emerging Industry Plan announced in

2012 aimed for China's chip design, chip manufacturing, packaging, and testing capabilities to "reach internationally advanced level" by 2020.

Clearly, this objective was not met. Some Chinese semiconductor companies may have reached "internationally advanced level" briefly, such as Huawei's HiSilicon, but it was highly vulnerable and unsustainable. Both Huawei HiSilicon and SMIC are struggling to maintain operations under U.S. sanctions that have severed their supplies.

The controversial "Made in China 2025" policy initiative, one that the Chinese government stopped publicizing after the U.S.-China trade dispute, intensified and targeted for 70 percent self-sufficiency for its chip demand by 2025.

Looking at various definitions of "self-sufficiency," China is far behind on this objective and is almost certain to miss it. Some Chinese media divide China's IC sales value by the value of China's chip imports to conclude a 36 percent self-sufficiency ratio in 2019.[153] But it confuses IC sales with IC production, two different concepts.

Moreover, it ignores that the vast majority of ICs manufactured in China were by non-Mainland China-headquartered companies like TSMC, SK Hynix, Samsung, and Intel. Considering that Mainland China-headquartered companies produced only 39 percent of China's total IC production, the self-sufficiency ratio was 6.1 percent in 2019,[154] hopelessly behind the 70 percent target in 2025.

Indeed, the industrial policy targets promulgated by Beijing were unrealistic and ignorant of related market-based economics. The semiconductor industry has long development cycles and requires enormous and persistent investment and focus. Attempts to make giant leaps forward in a short time span are destined to fail. Yet, the bureaucrats and engineers inside the Chinese government appear to have not learned this lesson.

That's why the shift in China's effort to seek self-sufficiency in semiconductors after the ZTE event in 2017 was game-changing. It was no longer government-driven but driven by private enterprises striving for their commercial survival. Therefore, it could portend a different outcome.

For SMIC, the changing external environment heralded the end of Qiu's stability and profitability strategy. As the window for relatively accessible U.S. supplies began to close, SMIC acted quickly. In May 2017, Qiu's CEO role was replaced by Zhao Haijun, a SMIC veteran with a Mainland background who was the chief operating officer before the new appointment.

The more important addition came six months later, as Liang Mengsong, a Taiwanese technology pioneer credited with leading important technological advances at both TSMC and Samsung, was named Co-CEO.

SMIC thus entered the era of co-CEOs with Zhao and Liang sharing the leadership position; this was another delicate arrangement balancing the Mainland Chinese and Taiwanese interests. This time, SMIC would race against time in the opposite direction: expanding and advancing technologically as rapidly as possible.

Liang's background made him the perfect person to lead this effort. An electronic engineering Ph.D. from the University of California at Berkeley, he joined TSMC in 1992 and had intimately participated in the company's R&D in each of the company's evolving manufacturing nodes.

Famously, Liang worked with his Ph.D. supervisor Yu Zhenhua, who was then TSMC's chief technology officer, to develop 130 nm manufacturing nodes based on TSMC's own technology in the early 2000s. It was viewed by the industry as a landmark win by TSMC to become a real competitor in the advanced chip manufacturing business. Moreover, Liang is the inventor of around 500 TSMC patents and is the most technologically capable expert in the industry.[155]

It's worthwhile to describe Liang's career experience before he joined SMIC in greater detail. His journey showed how talent flow was perhaps the most critical way for transferring advanced technology and know-how across national borders. It is a much more effective and efficient method of technology transfer than "forced technology transfer" via joint ventures.

In 2009, Liang left TSMC after 17 years, with some speculating the cause was losing his fight for a top R&D leadership role. After the expiration of a two-year non-compete clause, Liang joined Samsung as chief technology officer of the Korean conglomerate's LSI Department or its semiconductor unit.

Liang quickly led Samsung to catch up with industry leader TSMC across several generations of manufacturing nodes. Eventually, Samsung was able to reach 16nm production earlier than TSMC.[156]

This dramatic closing of the technology gap between TSMC and Samsung alerted TSMC, which sued Liang in 2014 in Taiwanese court for infringement of business secrets in a civil lawsuit.

TSMC alleged Liang might have "continually leaked TMSC's business secrets to Samsung" when he joined South Korea's Sungkyunkwan University, a close private entity with a close partnership with Samsung. Moreover, TSMC alleged that Liang taught private classes at an internal Samsung training center inside Samsung, with the students being veteran Samsung technology experts. The teaching position was, in fact, a cover for Liang to stay within the bounds of his non-compete agreement with TSMC.[157]

To make this arrangement more appealing, the Korean company offered Liang a compensation package more than triple what he earned at TSMC. And to entice Liang and his team members who later joined Samsung, the Korean company frequently used its corporate jet to shuttle them between Taiwan and South Korea.[158]

The most critical evidence was a report commissioned by TSMC comparing the product key process structures among TSMC, Samsung, and IBM. An external expert team used a state-of-the-art electron microscope to analyze the tiny transistors of one ten-thousandth of a hair to compare the main structural features of the latest four generations of the products of the three companies, as well as the constituent materials.

The team found that around 2009, Samsung's 65 nm process had features similar to IBM's and very different from TSMC. It was expected because Samsung's technology originated from IBM. But after 2009, when Liang began teaching at Sungkyunkwan University, Samsung's 45nm, 32nm, and 28nm nodes showed a diminishing difference from TSMC's technology. The report listed seven key transistor process characteristics and stated that the shape of the shallow trench isolation layer and the material combination of the back dialectic layer were all highly similar to TSMC's products.

Moreover, the report found that the silicon-germanium compound of Samsung's 28nm process P-type transistor electrode is more similar to the diamond-shaped structure of TSMC and is completely different from IBM's U-shaped disk. Samsung's 16nm and 14nm FinFET products were even impossible to be distinguished from TSMC's products through structural analysis. These "fingerprint" features, TSMC claimed, showed that Liang leaked TSMC's business secrets to Samsung.

TSMC asked the Taiwanese court to stop Liang from leaking its business secrets to Samsung, including TSMC's R&D personnel information. It also asked the court to prohibit Liang from working or providing any services in any means to Samsung before the end of 2015.

After an initial rejection from the court, TSMC won the case in 2015 after an appeal.[159] But it was of little consequence, as Liang already joined Samsung in 2011 and worked there for four years, and formulated Samsung's technology counterattack. When the verdict came from Taiwan's highest court in August 2015, it was only four months until Liang could legally work for Samsung.[160]

Taiwanese media called Liang Mengsong a "traitor" who shook up the island's economic foundation. "Taiwan's global foothold in the technology industry, coupled with the recent race by Mainland China to catch up technologically via unscrupulous means, has made the issue of (technological) 'traitors' increasingly important. One article commented that it is almost to the point of 'losing one person to lose the nation'".[161]

The exclamation is not an overstatement. It showed how technology transfer across national borders via the flow of top experts was extremely potent. Liang's experience at SMIC would again prove this point. As TSMC's chief legal consul Fang Shuhua said in 2015: " Even if (Liang) didn't actively leak TSMC secrets, he just needed to tell Samsung to not go toward a certain direction when Samsung tried to decide its R&D efforts would save Samsung an enormous amount of energy and time."[162]

Furthermore, since the flow of top experts – the human capital - cannot be stopped completely, technology transfer will always be part of the development of the global technology industry. This process is regulated and protected by a myriad of international and national intellectual property laws but also intertwined with geopolitical conflicts and corporate might.

Specifically, TSMC's lawsuit against Liang was very similar to TSMC's legal challenge of Richard Chang, the founder of SMIC, a decade previous. But TSMC didn't sue Samsung in the U.S. to repeat the lethal defeat it successfully achieved against SMIC because "compared to SMIC back then, Samsung's corporate scale and product lines are much bigger and complicated…the consequences are unpredictable if we starts the (legal) fight," said TSMC's chief legal consul Fang Shuhua.[163]

Sometimes, prolonged legal proceedings lasting for years can make the protection arrive too late to remedy damages that have already been caused. In TSMC's lawsuit against SMIC, lawyers raised the possibility that if the proceedings had lasted for years, even if TSMC won the case, the verdict would be a moot point if SMIC had advanced to next-generation technology.

With this background explained, the implication of Liang's joining SMIC was clearly significant. It was a big win for SMIC to recruit Liang, particularly at a time when SMIC was revving on all cylinders to advance its technology.

Liang didn't waste time to demonstrate his worth. SMIC was encountering great problems trying to develop its 28nm nodes. In February 2016, SMIC announced that its 28nm nodes had entered the critical tape-out phase, but the yield had been very inconsistent. After Liang joined SMIC, he and his team used less than one year to improve SMIC's yield of its 28nm nodes to over 85 percent from around 3 percent previously.[164]

But 28nm wasn't technologically leading at that time. Other Chinese foundries reached the same milestone, and TSMC's factory in Nanjing city planned to launch volume production of 16nm nodes in 2018.

Liang again chose an ambitious development path: to develop the most advanced technology while jumping across several generations. TSMC developed 22nm and 20nm nodes after 28nm and then reached 16/12nm technology. Liang decided that SMIC would jump from 28nm to develop 14nm nodes directly.

In August 2018, SMIC announced that it had achieved trial production of 14nm modes by partnering with companies including China-based Huawei and U.S.-based Qualcomm. But the yield was still very low. Liang and his team used another ten months to improve the yield from 3 percent to over 95 percent in 2019, and this signaled the formal volume production of 14nm nodes.[165] The team was also working on developing 12nm and 7nm nodes, the leading technology that only a few companies (TSMC, Samsung, and Intel) in the world were daring to do.

This advance was halted in 2020 as U.S.-China trade and tech frictions deepened. In October that year, SMIC announced that the Bureau of Industry and Security of the U.S. Department of Commerce had issued letters to suppliers that SMIC had been designated as a "military end-user." Certain U.S. equipment, parts, and raw materials exported to SMIC would be further restricted by U.S. export control regulations.

Two months later, SMIC and some of its subsidiaries were included in the U.S. "entity list" on the grounds of protecting U.S. national security. In accordance with U.S. export control regulations, suppliers would need to obtain an export license from the U.S. Department of Commerce before they could supply SMIC with items subject to regulations. A "presumptive rejection" policy meant such licenses should be expected to be rejected.

At the same time, SMIC and over 100 Chinese companies were included in December 2020 on the U.S. list of Chinese companies linked to the Chinese military. The list, which was a culmination of a program based on a mixture of presidential executive orders and public laws,[166] restricted Americans from trading SMIC stocks and derivatives.

For SMIC, these sanctions had a significant impact on its operations. Most of its main material and equipment suppliers are overseas companies, and there are few substitutes available. The company faced the risk of a shortage of production materials and therefore could not continue certain productions. Moreover, for items dedicated to the production of 10nm and below technology nodes, the U.S. Department of Commerce adopted a "presumptive rejection" policy, meaning SMIC's path toward technological advances would be blocked.

The most salient example is SMIC's failed attempt to purchase an extreme ultraviolet lithography machine (EUV) from Dutch company ASML Holding NV. This machine is needed for manufacturing the most advanced chips, including 7nm and lower (more advanced) nodes.

In 2018, SMIC reportedly signed a contract to purchase an EUV machine from ASML. But under U.S. government pressure, the Dutch government declined to renew a license needed for shipping it.

In February 2021, SMIC said it had signed a revised contract to purchase DUV machines, which are less advanced and incapable of achieving advanced chip manufacturing, from ASML.[167]

Without EUV machines, SMIC can't continue its development trajectory. As TSMC successfully entered volume production of 5nm nodes in 2020 and is expected to reach volume production of 3nm nodes in the second half of 2022, SMIC finds its 7nm node development in jeopardy.

Moreover, in March 2021, it was reported that SMIC had received licenses to import equipment from certain U.S. companies for mature processes. Industry insiders expect that the restrictions on advanced technologies would be kept in place for SMIC.[168]

This suggests that the U.S. is adopting a "hedging" strategy in its technology policy toward China. It is very similar to the U.S. attempt to balance commercial interests with national security on export control for the past few decades. In the case of SMIC, the U.S. is trying to balance commercial interests with the technology containment of China.

Whether SMIC's operations involve China's military is a subject of debate. Before the Trump administration placed SMIC on the export control scheme, it circulated a research report produced by defense contractor SOS International LLC, stating that SMIC aids China's defense establishment.

The report said that SMIC had worked with one of China's largest defense conglomerates. Its smoking gun was its allegation that researchers at universities linked to China's military had designed their work to fit SMIC technology. Some who read the report believed that the evidence was not enough to label SMIC as a military-linked company, while others claimed that SMIC was deeply embedded in China's defense industry research projects.[169] SMIC, of course, argued that its products were solely for civilian and commercial uses.

If taking into account the fundamental transformation previously described that "dual-use has become the rule and not the exception," the effort to control dual-use goods is a conflicted endeavor from the outset.

If dual-use goods are the rule, then it entails that a large majority of goods should be controlled. But that is obviously not realistic or practical.

In addition, semiconductors used for military purposes are generally mature technology. The most advanced chips, such as 7nm or more advanced, are used mostly for consumer goods such as smartphones. To limit SMIC's ability on advanced technology would do little to impact China's military. Therefore, the policy toward SMIC is designed to thwart the company's technological advances so that the U.S. can maintain its technological stranglehold on China in a critical industrial sector.

For SMIC, the company's operations face significant uncertainties. "We are working very hard with our suppliers. And our suppliers, majority are long-term partnership, has been working with SMIC for about 20 years. So we understand each other. We trust each other. So at this moment, we're working hard to apply the licenses, work closely with U.S. government…And the suppliers are working very, very closely with SMIC and the U.S. government…We work hard to build out the trust, to get it through," SMIC's Co-CEO Zhao Haijun said during an earnings call in February 2021.[170]

For many years, the unstated U.S. policy had been to keep China at least two generations behind global state-of-the-art semiconductor manufacturing capabilities. That's why in the early 2000s when the U.S. felt that China had narrowed the gap too much between the U.S. and Chinese semiconductor manufacturing technology– purportedly from 10 years in the 1980s to two years or less in 2002 - it prompted a government policy review of its export control scheme.[171]

Going forward, the U.S. is likely to continue this "hedging" strategy by allowing SMIC to function at less advanced nodes but cutting off its access to advanced technology. The U.S. needs to keep the Sword of Damocles swinging above SMIC's neck and above the Chinese semiconductor sector.

4. Huawei HiSilicon

Huawei is HiSilicon, and HiSilicon is Huawei.

- anonymous Huawei Insider

4.1 The Success And Curse Of Being Bundled

Many people became aware of Huawei's semiconductor unit HiSilicon at the outset of U.S. sanctions against Huawei around 2019, but few people know that the Chinese telecommunications company's semiconductor ambitions started humbly nearly three decades previous. In 1991, just four years after Huawei was established, founder Ren Zhengfei established an ASIC Design Center[172] with the objective of developing chips for the company's core product: telephone exchange switches.

During the first several years of Huawei's business in the late 1980s, it mainly resold private branch exchange (PBX) switches imported from Hong Kong to mainland Chinese organizations like hotels wanting to install telephone systems. To lower costs and offer more competitive rates, Huawei began purchasing parts and assembling the switches by itself a few years later.

The strategy worked, and Ren decided to double down: Huawei would develop its own parts and sell products under its own brand. That decision led to the establishment of Huawei's ASIC Design Center. The move was based on Ren's belief that owning core technology capabilities and more of the supply chain was critical to the company's long-term development.

In 1991, Ren began searching for talent to develop a chip for Huawei's core product, C&C08 switches. With around 50 staff, Huawei was a young and unknown company but growing rapidly as demand for telephone systems exploded across the country. Still, it took great effort for Ren to convince an engineer named Xu Wenwei from a small Hong Kong electronics telecommunications equipment company called Elite Industrial Holdings Ltd. to join Huawei. Xu led a small team of engineers in a dilapidated industrial building on the outskirts of Shenzhen as they toiled on the project. In 1993, Huawei successfully launched a self-developed digital ASIC chip, SD509. It was just able to perform the core functions required by switches and therefore reduce costs for Huawei's products.[173]

Huawei's semiconductor unit was critical to the success of the company's main telecommunications business. Because Huawei could use its own chips, which were often the most expensive part of its final products, the company could offer lower prices than rivals who relied on chips from suppliers.

As semiconductor research work intensified, Huawei purchased foreign EDA (Electronic Design Automation) software[174], the essential but pricy tools for designing integrated circuits and printed circuit boards. It was an important big investment in semiconductor research and a rare move by a Chinese company at that time. It demonstrated Huawei's determination to self-design chips for its own products for the long term.

In fact, during the first decade of Huawei's development, the company already became an outlier in the amount it spent on R&D. In 1996, Huawei's R&D intensity[175] reached 6.9 percent.[176] As a comparison, the average R&D intensity of China's information technology sector was only 5.3 percent 22 years later in 2018, and the information technology sector had the highest R&D intensity among all industries in China. Other sectors like healthcare had an average R&D intensity of around 3 percent in 2018.

Huawei's R&D intensity would grow steadily over the years to 13.86 percent in 2018. An oft-overlooked fact is that Huawei's total R&D expenditure in 2018 was more than that of Alibaba, Baidu, and Tencent – the three largest Chinese Internet companies – combined.[177] In 2016, Huawei's R&D expenditure alone accounted for 7 percent of all Chinese corporate R&D expenditure and was more than the combined total of all overseas-listed Chinese companies.[178] Huawei also ranked as the only Chinese company and the sixth on the world's top 20 companies in terms of R&D expenditure in 2018, just behind Amazon, Alphabet, Volkswagen, Samsung, and Microsoft.[179]

Huawei's focus on R&D and its aim to be self-reliant was firmly established in its early days and was consistent for decades. As the company grew, it continuously improved its R&D framework. In 1995, Huawei streamlined its R&D operations, setting up a Central Research Department with multiple sub-departments under its umbrella. One sub-department was the Basic Research unit, which was responsible for designing chips for Huawei's telecommunications equipment.

This unit designed many types of chips, including analog circuit SA series, digital circuit SD series, and thick film circuit SD series, covering core technologies such as program-controlled switches, optical transmission, and WCDMA base stations. The Basic Research unit expanded rapidly along with Huawei's main telecommunications business. With over 300 chip design engineers by the end of the 1990s[180], Huawei's chip unit might have become China's biggest and most advanced chip design team.

Comparing to other semiconductor companies in China, the most unique characteristic of HiSilicon was that it was bundled with Huawei's end-product team. Because of China's semiconductor industry history, there were no real integrated device manufacturers (IDM) in China. Most Chinese semiconductor companies focused on designing or manufacturing chips and then selling their services or products to third-party clients. But HiSilicon provided its products to Huawei directly, therefore linking the chip design team intimately with the end-product team. If Huawei had in-house chip manufacturing capabilities, it would have become a formidable IDM. But Huawei didn't take this final step as explained in the earlier chapter.

The benefits of bundling the chip design team and the end-product team were enormous and critical: the two teams could work together on a daily basis and push each other to advance technologically in parallel. It made rapid chip reiteration possible, offering Huawei abilities to upgrade its products to be more competitive while improving HiSilicon's chip design sophistication at the same time.

From the 1990s to the early 2000s, Huawei successfully developed 100,000-gate, million-gate, and tens of millions-gate ASIC chips that facilitated its end-product upgrades.[181] It led to explosive sales of Huawei's switches product, C&C08. In 1998, C&C08 sold 10.7 million lines; but in 2003, it sold 25 million lines, and there were over 130 million lines cumulatively running on the global telecom network.[182] It was a cycle where more sales led to more capital available for R&D, which led to technological advances that helped generate faster sales growth.

This was in stark contrast to the decoupled condition of China's electronics and semiconductor sectors. Because the Chinese electronics industry relied on imported chips, Chinese semiconductor companies didn't have an opportunity to test their products and evolve their technology. It then reinforced the electronic companies' reliance on foreign chips. This vicious cycle was very hard to break.

As Huawei's business expanded rapidly, its sales grew 2.6 times, and the number of staff almost doubled from 1999 to 2003[183], and it made more organizational changes to its chip unit. Based on Huawei's ASIC Design Center, HiSilicon Technologies was registered in 2004 as a new company with independent operations and became a subsidiary of Huawei.

Over a decade later, Huawei executives explained that internally, there had always been two "HiSilicon." "Big HiSilicon" designed chips for Huawei products only. Huawei's Kirin phone processors, Balong baseband chips, Tiangang 5G base station chips, Ascend AI chips, and Kunpeng server chips were within this category. "Small HiSilicon" designed chips that could be sold to other companies. Huawei's video surveillance chips IPCam, MobileCam chips, STB chips for set-top boxes, TV SoC chips, and NB-IoT chips fell under this category.[184]

When and how the division between "Big HiSilicon" and "Small HiSilicon" took place is unclear. The distinction was also not set in stone as Huawei said in 2019 that it would sell its phone and 5G chips to third parties.[185] For convenience, we will use HiSilicon to refer to Huawei's overall chip unit during its early development.

HiSilicon's establishment in 2004 was no coincidence as it took place at the dawn of 3G development and the mobile Internet era. Huawei had built its mobile phone department the year before, and this later became the company's high-profile growth engine: Huawei Consumer Business Group.

Moreover, Huawei just had a record-breaking year in 2003. The company scored global sales of US$3.83 billion, with international sales rising a whopping 90 percent year-on-year. It took over 40% of China's domestic telecommunications equipment bidding projects by China Telecom and China Netcom and won the second position in the worldwide xDSL market based on equipment shipment.[186]

From a position of strength and security of its main telecommunication business, Huawei finally decided – after much hesitation - to enter the hot mobile phone market. Ren Zhengfei had repeatedly said that Huawei would never enter the terminal device business, but ultimately the opportunity was deemed too great to ignore. Initially, HiSilicon and Huawei's mobile phone department – both newly established entities - were separate units trying to tackle the mobile phone market with their own separate strategies.

In 2004, Huawei released its first phones: U626 and A616. Both were low-cost customized models for telecom operators. For HiSilicon, it was evident that the mass adoption of the mobile phone would drive up demand for phone chips, and it decided first to develop GSM Turnkey solutions to meet the rising demand for conventional button mobile phones in the Chinese market.

In 2006, HiSilicon began developing the product. It took three years, which was in line with industry averages, to complete the GSM Turnkey solution by 2009. The application process (AP) chip was called K3V1, using the manufacturing process of 110 nm. But the chip didn't achieve much traction, as phone makers in China didn't want to use it.

K3V1 wasn't competitive with rivals like MediaTek Inc's more mature product that had been dominating the Chinese market. In addition, the chip wasn't tested yet and wasn't advanced in terms of the manufacturing process as competitors were already using 45nm to 65 nm nodes. Moreover, Huawei's solution used the Windows Mobile operating system, an OS that was being increasingly marginalized.

What's important to understand is that HiSilicon was an independent subsidiary of Huawei at this point and responsible for its own financial performance. It produced the K3V1 solutions to target all phone makers and compete with rival products like MediaTek chips on the market. But outside of a few small copycat low-end phone makers in Shenzhen, HiSilicon couldn't convince other phone makers to use its chips.[187] The cycle of Chinese electronics companies relying on better and more mature non-Chinese chips wasn't going to be easily broken by HiSilicon.

The failure of the K3V1 chip, however, paved the way for HiSilicon's future success. It led to a critical decision by Huawei to transfer HiSilicon's mobile device chip business to Huawei's mobile phone unit, therefore bundling the chip and phone businesses.

According to a company insider, executives had different ideas about how to go about developing HiSilicon's mobile device products. In the end, founder Ren Zhengfei determined that for HiSilicon to tackle the consumer electronics chips business alone wouldn't work. Not only did HiSilicon have no experience, but the costs would also be enormous and the potential return highly uncertain. There were also high entry barriers that created many strong and experienced competitors.

Keeping the tradition of using internally designed chips, Huawei's leadership decided that its phone unit would use HiSilicon chips. In return, the phone unit would compensate HiSilicon for its R&D costs. This way, the interests of the two units were aligned. HiSilicon would have one guaranteed client, while the phone unit would only source chips from HiSilicon.[188]

This arrangement did turn out to be the critical piece of the puzzle for HiSilicon's eventual success that came over a decade later. Based on the lessons learned from K3V1, HiSilicon worked to improve its chips and released the K3V2 processor in 2012. It used ARM architecture, 40 nm nodes, and supported the Android operating system instead of Windows Mobile, which put it much more in line with mainstream chips.

Huawei claimed it to be the smallest quad-core processor in the industry.[189] Another big difference this time was that K3V2 didn't have to struggle to find a client. The processor was used on Huawei Ascend D1 quad-core version phones released in a high-profile release event in 2012 on the eve of the Mobile World Congress in Barcelona, Spain.

The K3V2 chips achieved significant improvements, but the process of putting the chip inside a flagship phone was filled with challenges. The chip faced persistent technical problems and threatened the firm's ability to meet the deadline's release date. The software team for the Huawei phone had to work day and night to compensate for the chip's many bugs.

Even with all this work, the chip still had critical weaknesses, including low power efficiency, a tendency for overheating, and weak compatibility with mobile gaming's needs. Not to mention it still lagged far behind rival products such as Qualcomm's Snapdragon S4 Pro processor APQ 8064 and Samsung Exynos 4412, which used 28 and 32 nm nodes and had a much better overall performance.

An engineer who witnessed the process of launching the first HiSilicon chips-equipped Huawei phone described it as "Huawei's phone unit racing toward the finishing line while pulling the arm of an out-ofbreath HiSilicon."[190] The chip design team faced more challenges than the phone unit and was only able to achieve basic functionality to meet the demand of the phone.

But by being deeply bundled with HiSilicon, Huawei's phone unit had to continue using the chip. Huawei's next flagship smartphone, the Ascend P6, was released in 2013 in a flashy global launch event in London and used an updated K3V2 processor. The launch of Ascend P6 was a significant push by Huawei's phone unit to move up to mid-range priced phones from the company's previous low-end phones.

The phone's selling point included being thinner than rivals and sporting many high-end hardware features on a mid-range priced device. The fact that this phone used processors designed by Huawei was barely mentioned or emphasized in the news coverage at the time. In 2013, no one could have foreseen the significance or implication of a Huawei phone using its own self-designed chips.

The focus of the public's attention was evaluating the phone based on its features and performance. In this regard, the improved K3V2 chip achieved its purpose: it didn't noticeably lower the phone's functionality and quality. The P6 phone was also a step upward for Huawei, having sold around four million units globally as of mid-2014.[191]

From then on, Huawei's phone and chips unit progressed concurrently. In 2014, Huawei released its Mate 7 phone, a first attempt at the high-end market. It used HiSilicon's newly named Kirin chip. Kirin is a mythical hooved Chinese chimerical creature, and it carried Huawei's hope that this chip would create miracles. The Kirin series chips began with Kirin 910 chips that were used on Huawei P6S phones and Kirin 920 chips used on Huawei Honor 6 phones. Both were unveiled in 2014 and achieved decent performances.

The Kirin chips were different from those created in the past because they integrated HiSilicon's self-developed baseband processor Balong chips to create an SoC (System on a Chip). The SoC later gradually integrated audio chips, video chips, and ISP (image signal processor) chips to improve performance. Integrating HiSilicon's other in-house expertise, including baseband processors, would become one of the hallmarks for Kirin chips, which helped differentiate Huawei phones from its competitors.

The real test came with Kirin 925 chips used by Huawei Mate 7 phones. Kirin chips had shown that they could support low-end and mid-range phones, but could they succeed in a high-end phone? The answer was positive.

The Kirin 925 chips can be said to have finally stood on par with international competitors. The chip used 28nm nodes, similar to industry leader Qualcomm's comparable chips. The power consumption efficiency and graphics process were improved to offer better gaming and video experience.

A comprehensive technical comparison showed that the Kirin chips were only slightly inferior to Qualcomm's chips,[192] and this was an unthinkable level for a Chinese chip design company to have reached. The Huawei Mate 7 phone sold over 7.5 million units globally and took a firm position in the world's high-end phone market.[193]

A decade after HiSilicon was established, its chips had finally narrowed the technology gap with industry-leading rivals. Next, HiSilicon set an even more ambitious goal: to design a phone chip that could perform as well or even better than industry leaders. This effort was interrupted in 2020 when U.S. sanctions made it impossible for HiSilicon to contract chip manufacturers to produce its chips, but HiSilicon was very close, or some would argue, had already achieved such an objective.

After the Kirin 925 chips, HiSilicon unveiled Kirin 950 chips used on Huawei's Mate 8 phones in 2015. The Kirin 950 chips achieved several milestones in terms of its performance. It had 17.14 percent faster CPU speed and 200 MHz faster GPU clock speed than Qualcomm's Snapdragon 810 MSM8994 and used 16 nm nodes, smaller than the 20 nm nodes used by Qualcomm's Snapdragon 810 MSM8994.[194] The chip also integrated HiSilicon's self-developed ISP, supporting superior camera functions that became one of Huawei phone's most outstanding selling features.

Even though Kirin 950 chips performed better in some functions, its overall performance still had a slightly lower score than Qualcomm's Snapdragon 810.[195] In addition, Qualcomm released its Snapdragon 820 chips a year later in 2016 to take back some lost ground. The Snapdragon 820 used 14 nm nodes and offered two times faster downloads than Kirin 950.

A behind-the-scene story recorded in a book composed by Huawei University showed the challenges of making the Kirin 950. In the autumn of 2015, when Mate 8 phone had already begun trial production, one inspector inadvertently discovered that the radio signals of two Mate 8 phones stacked on top of each other would immediately be lost because they canceled each other out. The RF (radio-frequency) module equipped for Kirin 950 was HiSilicon's self-developed 4G RF chip. It was an unexpected error unlikely to be discovered if not for how intensely the inspectors had been testing the Mate 8 phones and therefore incidentally stacked the phones.

The RF chip teams spent two months finding out where the problems originated. Finally, they determined that it was a mistake in the design because a layer of the mask was missing. The mistake was only in one patch of volume production chips, and the next patch didn't have this error. HiSilicon scrapped the bad batch of chips and 60,000 Mate 8 phones that were already made equipped with the flawed chips.[196]

Another sign of HiSilicon's technological sophistication was that it was the first to achieve volume production of an industry-leading manufacturing process. Kirin 950 adopted 16nm FinFET Plus process and was the first to achieve volume production of chips using this process around mid-2015.[197]

Each time the semiconductor industry inches forward with smaller nodes to have more transistors on the chip, the cooperation between the chip designer and chip manufacturer is critical. To achieve this, HiSilicon started negotiating and working with TSMC, its chip manufacturing partner, as early as 2013.

For TSMC, it took on certain risks to work with HiSilicon because the company didn't have prior experience as the first to adopt advanced manufacturing processes. It was a test for HiSilicon's technological capabilities, expertise, and subsequent commercial application of the chip. Instead of following in the footsteps of others, HiSilicon had to explore a new path through hundreds of processing steps in partnership with TSMC. It was a stressful time for both TSMC and HiSilicon. At certain times, there would be tens of thousands of warnings in the code logs. Engineers had to go through all the warnings one by one over many sleepless nights.[198]

From 2016, HiSilicon unveiled one new flagship chip each year. The Kirin 960, 970, 980, 990 chips were released annually between 2016 and 2019. These chips can be said to be industry-leading and helped Huawei achieve outstanding performance for its high-end phone business.

Contrary to the early years of HiSilicon, when Huawei's phone unit had to pull HiSilicon by the hand to meet the growth speed of the phone business, HiSilicon was now one of the major competitive edges for Huawei phones. Huawei is one of three major phone makers in the world that also designs their own chips, besides Apple Inc. and Samsung. This gives Huawei flexibility and in-house capabilities to compete with the world's most powerful phone makers.

At its peak, HiSilicon briefly became one of the world's top 10 largest semiconductor companies. During the first six months of 2020, HiSilicon's sales were estimated to be $5.2 billion, ranking tenth globally in terms of semiconductor sales, after industry giants Intel ($38.95 billion), Samsung ($29.75 billion), TSMC ($20.72 billion), SK Hynix ($13.09

billion), Micron (US$10.62 billion), Broadcom (US$8.11 billion), Qualcomm ($7.86 billion), Nvidia ($6.53 billion), and Texas Instruments ($6.24 billion).[199]

HiSilicon would have also become one of the top 5 fabless chip design companies in the world in 2020 if it were to maintain its sales growth. For the whole year of 2020 (the numbers above were for the first half of 2020), the world's top 5 largest fabless companies were Qualcomm ($19.41 billion), Broadcom ($17.75 billion), Nvidia ($15.41 billion), MediaTek ($10.93 billion), and AMD ($9.76 billion).[200] HiSilicon would have come close to making the top 5 list if not for U.S. sanctions severing its supply chain.

Within China, HiSilicon's dominant position is even more pronounced. During the first quarter of 2020, HiSilicon took 43.9 percent of the Chinese smartphone SoC market, followed by Qualcomm's 32.8 percent and MediaTek's 13.1 percent.[201] For AP (application processor) shipments alone, HiSilicon accounted for 20 percent of total handset AP demand in China in 2019.[202]

In parallel to HiSilicon's growth was Huawei phone's entry into the ranks of the global top three phone makers. Huawei briefly became the world's largest phone maker in the second quarter of 2020[203] but was quickly eclipsed by rivals. Of course, these numbers from HiSilicon and Huawei were distorted after 2019 when U.S. sanctions disrupted its normal operations.

Outside of phone chips, HiSilicon products have taken a large market share in other categories. HiSilicon was estimated to have a 60% global market share and 70% of the domestic Chinese market for video surveillance chips. HiSilicon also shipped over ten million chips for major 4K TV brands like Sharp as early as 2016, and HiSilicon claimed to be able to ship one million of its Boudica 120 chips used for smart city projects every month in 2017.[204] In the first quarter of 2020, HiSilicon's baseband chips accounted for 20 percent of the global market.[205]

But these categories are much smaller markets compared to smartphone chips. For example, the baseband chip market was $26.8 billion in 2020, and the shipments are much smaller for unit numbers. In comparison, Qualcomm's 2020 fiscal revenue was $23.5 billion, and 77 percent of its revenues were phone-related.[206] The global shipment of phones stood at 1.38 billion in 2020, and the related phone chip shipments are normally counted in the unit of a million or more.

It was clear that without U.S. sanctions, the Huawei phone would have become a formidable competitor to Apple and Samsung, and HiSilicon would be one of the world's top fabless firms. Then decisions from Washington, D.C., stopped everything.

4.2 The U.S.'s Trump Card

On May 16, 2019, the U.S. placed Huawei on its Entity List and this limited Huawei's access to U.S. technology.[207] The U.S. export control laws have wide-ranging extraterritorial reach. They can restrict the movement of not only U.S. technology but also non-U.S. components that contain U.S. technology. For example, after Huawei was placed on the Entity List, any product made by any company around the world needed to ensure their products didn't contain more than a certain percentage of U.S. technology, normally understood to be 25 percent, in order to continue supplying Huawei.[208]

This change meant that U.S. chipmakers such as Intel, Qualcomm, Xilinx, and Broadcom could not sell to Huawei immediately after the ban unless they obtained a license. Understandably, their products would certainly contain more than 25 percent U.S. technology. But TSMC determined that it could continue manufacturing chips for Huawei because "its technology symposium...does not have over 25% U.S.-origin technology in its manufacturing process."[209]

The reasoning was supported by the fact that TSMC had around 90 percent of labor and overhead in Taiwan; a substantial portion of its blank silicon wafers were from Japan, Europe, and Taiwan. The U.S. portion in TSMC's manufacturing process included EDA software (for designing chips), intellectual property, and equipment that were estimated to fall under 25 percent.[210]

The Entity List ban strangled Huawei's ability to purchase chips from certain suppliers, but the overall impact was controllable. Huawei could rely more on HiSilicon for its chip demand. Around 90 percent of HiSilicon's sales go to its parent company Huawei, and HiSilicon could expand its scope into developing more types of chips for Huawei. Most importantly, HiSilicon could still contract TSMC to manufacture its chips. So long as HiSilicon chips could be made, Huawei could maintain a steady supply of chips, albeit having to change the composition of its chip suppliers. Its smartphone business operations, which accounted for 54 percent of Huawei's revenues in 2019, could continue to operate.[211]

Huawei held out hope that it could negotiate with the U.S. government to ease the restriction. Meanwhile, it stocked up on chips and other materials in preparation for wartime. In 2019, Huawei spent $23.4 billion to stock up on chips, parts, and materials, up 73 percent from a year earlier. Huawei reportedly stocked up on a range of chips, including Field Programmable Gate Arrays (FPGAs) essential to its base station and telecommunication equipment rooms, DRAM and NAND flash memory chips, as well as high-end CPUs.

These were the type of chips that Huawei had relied on third-party suppliers and in which HiSilicon wasn't so strong. It also built up inventory via regulatory loopholes, such as using local chip distributors, traders, and its own suppliers to buy chips at far higher prices but ultimately transferred to be used by Huawei.[212]

The most deadly blow came a year later as new restrictions were announced on May 15, 2020. The U.S. government levied new restrictions on Huawei's supply chain. The most important change was that the 25 percent minimum U.S. technology rule was replaced by targeting any product containing any U.S. technology.[213]

TSMC could no longer continue making chips for HiSilicon because its manufacturing process contained U.S. technology. The percentage of U.S. technology didn't matter. U.S. technology was so critical in the global semiconductor supply chain that this new restriction meant that almost no foundries could manufacture chips for HiSilicon without a license. The new rule had a 120-day buffer period, and September 14 was the deadline for compliance with the new restriction.

Then on August 17, the U.S. added 38 Huawei subsidiaries to the entity list to have a total of 152 Huawei-related entities on the control list. It specified that no company in the world could sell any product containing U.S. technology to Huawei in any phase of any transaction. This closed the loophole for Huawei to purchase chips via distributors, traders, and suppliers or any other means to get around the ban. Huawei could no longer buy chips from others.

Under the new restrictions, all major semiconductor companies, including TSMC, Intel, Qualcomm, MediaTek, Micro Technology, and even China-based SMIC, couldn't supply Huawei after September 15. These new restrictions were essentially a death sentence for HiSilicon. It turned Huawei's chip supply chain from a flowing river to a dying pond that survived on saved inventories without any new inflows.

In the summer of 2020, Huawei's CEO of its consumer product business, Yu Chengdong, said, "Unfortunately, Huawei only entered chip design, not chip manufacturing…(The Kirin 9000 chip on Huawei Mate 40) might be the last generation of Kirin high-end chips." A month earlier, Ren Zhengfei said that "(now) we realized that some politicians in the U.S. wanted us to die."[214]

It is not an overstatement. HiSilicon, as a chip design firm, would wither if its products couldn't be manufactured and utilized in end-products. It would not only become an invalid business but also not able to advance technologically. Without the supply of chips, Huawei's smartphone business couldn't survive.

Indeed, Huawei's smartphone shipments have dropped from the world's second-largest vendor after Samsung with 17 percent global market share in 2019, falling out of the top five ranking companies in the first quarter of 2021. [215] Even within China, Huawei's smartphone shipment dropped 65 percent year-on-year in May 2021, and it lost its glory of being the absolute industry leader domestically for years.[216] In November 2020, Huawei presented its low-end phone unit, Honor, in order for it to survive independently.

HiSilicon was hit hard too. Its sales dropped 87 percent during the first quarter of 2021 compared to its peak sales during the second quarter of 2020.[217] It has not been able to manufacture its chips after September 15, 2020. But Huawei has repeatedly said that it wouldn't give up HiSilicon even if its chips couldn't be made. In Huawei executives' words, "Huawei is HiSilicon, and HiSilicon is Huawei."[218] Without one of them, the other wouldn't be the same.

As of the summer of 2021, HiSilicon said that its 7,000-people team was still on track to develop high-end chips as previously planned. HiSilicon was reportedly developing a 3nm chip potentially named Kirin 9010.[219] This would be the most cutting-edge technology in chip design, as TSMC expects 3nm nodes to achieve multiple customer product tape-outs in 2021 and is targeting volume production in the second half of 2022. In addition, HiSilicon is reportedly still hiring top fresh graduates to replenish its talent pool.

At nearly no financial return, the cost of such an effort was a huge burden for Huawei. The cost to keep HiSilicon running is measured at billions of U.S. dollars a year.[220] Understandably, Huawei wouldn't give up nearly two decades of expertise accumulation and industry-leading capabilities in one of the most critical sectors. Huawei will likely continue supporting HiSilicon for as long as it can, but for how long is highly uncertain.

There are a couple of scenarios in which HiSilicon could be salvaged. First and the least likely is that the manufacturing capabilities unavailable to HiSilicon could somehow be restored. It is hard to imagine how this could materialize, barring a significant improvement of U.S.-China relations in the post-Trump Biden administration. The probability for this to happen appears low.

The second scenario is to build non-U.S. chip manufacturing capabilities to manufacture HiSilicon chips. In other words, HiSilicon would become an IDM (integrated device manufacturer), designing, manufacturing, and selling its own chips. As explained earlier, HiSilicon didn't enter chip manufacturing because it made the decision consistent with the global industry trend of labor division between chip design and chip manufacturing. Now, that trend is reversing as the U.S., China, and Europe are all geared towards moving chip manufacturing capabilities onshore.

So Huawei is reportedly creating a dedicated chip manufacturing plant in Shanghai that uses no American technology. It would initially experiment with making mature nodes of 45nm chips and progress gradually toward more advanced chips. Reportedly, this plant would attempt to make 28nm chips by the end of 2021 and produce 20nm chips by late 2022.[221]

Such a timetable may be overly ambitious. The "dark magic" of the chip manufacturing process involves as many as 700 steps utilizing dozens of pieces of highly complex equipment. To have non-U.S. technology substitutes for all these equipment, materials, and processes will take time. In fact, this had never been tried before in such a highly globalized industry, and the unforeseen challenges are beyond imagination.

But for Huawei, this is a necessary step towards self-reliance. Its investment arm has invested in nearly 40 semiconductor-related companies since 2019, covering a wide range of the semiconductor supply chain, including EDA software, testing, packaging, materials, and equipment.[222] Clearly, Huawei couldn't cover every single step of the manufacturing process on its own. Its investments, therefore, aim to create an aligned supply chain centered around HiSilicon that could grow together toward self-sufficiency.

At the same time, Huawei is betting on third-generation semiconductors. The term refers to products based on a different type of semiconductor material (silicon carbide or gallium nitride) that features fast switching speed, small size, high efficiency, and fast heat dissipation. They have advantages in high-growth future applications such as 5G communications, autonomous vehicles, high-speed rail, robotics, satellite communications, and aerospace. Huawei has invested in a number of companies in this area and is hoping to build its foothold in a potentially future-changing technology. But the space is still in the early stages of development and could take many years to reach mature commercialization.

And thus, it will take years for Huawei to generate a successful, self-sufficient chip manufacturing capability absent of American technology. Such capabilities will be of low and mature technology at first and then take many more years to advance. For the type of high-end chips HiSilicon is designing, there won't be any quick solution. Can Huawei keep burning billions to support HiSilicon for years or even decades to come? It looks to be a tough prospect.

U.S. sanctions against Huawei that were based on American national security concerns – former President Trump claimed in October 2019 that "Huawei is a big concern of our military, our intelligence agencies and we are not doing business with Huawei"[223] – produced two colossal commercial collateral downfalls: HiSilicon, potentially one of the most advanced and biggest fabless companies; and Huawei's smartphone business, once a formidable competitor to Apple and Samsung.

And this is on top of Huawei's significantly damaged 5G ambitions. The U.S. and its allies such as Australia, Japan, and the U.K. and big markets like India and Vietnam have banned or avoided using Huawei equipment for their 5G networks. Without a solution to find new supplies of chips, even Huawei's 5G business could face disruptions as its chip inventory dries up.

In November 2020, the U.S. permitted Qualcomm to sell 4G mobile chips to Huawei. In July 2021, after repeated delays, Huawei released its newest phone, the P50 series, equipped partially with the Kirin 9000 and partially with the Qualcomm Snapdragon 888 4G chip.[224] At a time when 5G phones are becoming the mainstream, Huawei's 4G phone wouldn't be appealing to consumers, but it is good news for U.S.-based Qualcomm to regain a lost client in Asia.

The Qualcomm license suggests that the U.S. policy remains one of "hedging": balancing commercial interests with national security concerns; supporting commercial interests while maintaining a U.S. technology stranglehold on China's tech ecosystem.

It means a complete decoupling or a reversal of policy is unlikely. And future decades could very well see a "muddling through," as companies and industries operate in highly uncertain geopolitical, regulatory, and commercial environments. This is a tech war that will have sporadic and unpredictable battles, and when viewed through generations of Chinese science and technology development, are but the latest volley in an ongoing chronicle of growth.

5. A War With No Winners

The belief in the value of scientific truth is not derived from nature but is a product of definite cultures.

- Max Weber[225]

One sentiment which is assimilated by the scientist from the very outset of his training pertains to the purity of science. Science must not suffer itself to become the handmaiden of theology or economy or state. The function of this sentiment is likewise to preserve the autonomy of science. For if such extra-scientific criteria of the value of science as presumable consonance with religious doctrines or economic utility or political appropriateness are adopted, science becomes acceptable only insofar as it meets these criteria. In other words, as the "pure science sentiment" is eliminated, science becomes subject to the direct control of other institutional agencies and its place in society becomes increasingly uncertain.

- Robert K. Merton[226]

The U.S.-China tech war is not one started with a manifesto from either side or with one defining moment; it's better defined as a war with sporadic barrages and unpredictable battles overlaying a steady hum of preparation. Some frontlines have already been drawn, especially regarding semiconductors, 5G, and artificial intelligence. These areas are seeing deepening decoupling between the two countries that is tearing apart decades of globalized supply chains.

For the global semiconductor sector, the Covid pandemic combined with the disrupted semiconductor supply chain due to sanctions and stocking-up efforts created unprecedented shortages of chips for everything from cars to consumer electronics. The ensuing disruptions to car factories and consumers awakened the public and policymakers. The basic logic of the industry suddenly changed. Market economics have given in to supply chain security. What made sense economically previously – such as outsourcing chip manufacturing to where costs can be minimized, and efficiency maximized – no longer made sense.

The popular wisdom became that the world depended on Taiwanese chips too much, and it "poses a threat to the global economy." The old adage that "Real men have fabs" became fabulous again.[227] The U.S., Europe, and Asia are all striving to have more chip manufacturing capabilities located within their own borders to secure their own semiconductor supply chains.

The U.S. Senate passed an Act in June 2021 allocating $250 billion to support U.S. innovation, including $52 billion to fund semiconductor research, design, and manufacturing.[228] The European Union wants to double its chip manufacturing output to 20 percent of the global market by 2030, as part of the Block's $800 billion coronavirus response fund with 20 percent of the money earmarked for tech investment.[229] China is targeting, unrealistically, to have domestically-made semiconductors meet as much as 70 percent of its semiconductor demand.[230]

These initiatives were often made based on countering the China threat. President Joe Biden promised to outspend China on innovation and infrastructure to prevent it from overtaking the U.S. to become the world's most powerful country.[231] "The Chinese Communist Party is working overtime on cyber, AI, and machine learning so that they can become the world's preeminent superpower. We can't let our foot off the gas," claimed Sen. Ben Sasse, R-Neb.[232]

But the reasoning is based on the false perception of the effectiveness of China's government policies in the semiconductor sector. Lawmakers appear to be listening to think tanks and analysts with little real-world experience on the ground. As seen in the previous chapters, decades of Chinese industrial policy failed to lessen China's reliance on foreign chips or generate persistent technological advances.

Moreover, even though China is singled out as the chief rival of the U.S. and therefore sits at the center of public attention, it should be noted that many countries have and are engaged in the same tactics, including subsidies; government support to domestic industries; government R&D funding; and other government-led incentives to develop their own semiconductor industries with varying degrees of intensity.

Government-sponsored research, industrial policies, and Japanese banks' injecting capital into Japanese semiconductor firms during industry downturns contributed to Japan's semiconductor success from the 1960s to 1980s.[233] In the case of Taiwan, a government-sponsored research body, tax subsidies, and policy incentives provided the needed environment for Taiwan's semiconductor industry to germinate and grow in the 1970s and 1980s.

The Korean government created industrial compounds for semiconductor production and housed state-sponsored research institutions, used import restrictions to protect domestic firms' market share, and limited foreign direct investment to help nurture the early development of its semiconductor industry.[234] Then in 2021, the Korean government announced plans to provide huge tax incentives and tax credits to Korean chip manufacturers and vowed to invest more than $450 billion before 2030 to create the world's largest semiconductor manufacturing complex.[235]

Such government support is widespread in other tech sectors too. Aside from well-known sizeable subsidies and financing support received by Huawei, Swedish export authorities provided some $10 billion in credit assistance for Sweden's tech-and-telecom sector as of 2018. Finland authorized $30 billion in annual export credit guarantees economy-wide from 2017.[236]

An annual review by The Organization for Economic Co-operation and Development (OECD) found that in 2020, 33 of the 37 OECD countries, 21 of 27 European Union countries offer tax relief for R&D expenditure, and the share of tax relief in total government support in the OECD area increased from 36 percent in 2006 to 56 percent in 2018.[237]

While such policies are common, the effectiveness of government support and industrial policy is a matter of intense debate. One study finds that while industrial policy in China improves output while it is in effect, there is no evidence of a persistent beneficial impact.[238] China's industrial policy targeting the shipbuilding industry was found to have mixed effectiveness.[239] Another study in Thailand finds that trade openness and R&D are more crucial in fostering firms' productivity than industrial policies.[240] Others find that industrial policies allocated to competitive sectors or that foster competition in a sector increase productivity growth in China.[241]

In the case of China's semiconductor sector, industrial policy has certainly not worked very well. One of the most important reasons for its failure to include the Western tech blockade, which directly and indirectly led to a series of chain reactions that helped to foster SMIC's ambiguous identity and its ensuing corporate infighting; as well as to limit the Chinese government's ability to coordinate industrial research and to restrict Chinese companies' ability to receive technology transfers as those in Taiwan, South Korea, and Japan were fortunate to have received.

The timing was another issue, as the industry missed some key development opportunities through the years. When some of the global chip manufacturing capabilities moved to Mainland China, Taiwan's competitive advantages in chip manufacturing were already very entrenched, making it extremely hard to catch up. Services at the lower-end of the value chain, like chip testing and packaging, were first migrated to Mainland China, where the Chinese industry is the strongest currently. But such migration has not moved up to higher-value segments.

Aside from not being able to coordinate industry R&D, the Chinese government's investment in the industry was also ill-spent. Government subsidies were not used to spur R&D but instead used to keep many "zombie" companies alive and caused companies to engage in price wars.

A review of the top 30 Chinese A-share listed semiconductor companies by revenues in 2017 showed that half of the companies received government subsidies equaling to more than 10 percent of their profit. Eight of them received subsidies as much as 50 percent of their profit, and five companies received subsidies worth more than their profit.[242] Years of government subsidies only allowed commercially unviable firms to survive rather than thrive.

In addition, government subsidies and incentives were used by semiconductor companies to engage in price wars to take more market share. Because local semiconductor companies were mostly engaged in mature and low-end technology, their customers were very price sensitive. This led to price wars as each semiconductor company wanted to sell more products to scale up. For the local governments, their focus was for these companies to pay more taxes and to provide local employment opportunities. There were no performance metrics measuring R&D success, which was irrelevant to the short-sighted government officials' career prospects.[243]

Going forward, the Chinese semiconductor industry will continue to face grave challenges on the path toward self-sufficiency. The much-discussed National Integrated Circuits Industry Development Investment Fund (the Fund), which is often quoted to show how much money Beijing is investing in the domestic chips sector, is investing in too many companies for an insufficient time length.

The Fund, with roughly $53 billion in capital, has invested in dozens of Chinese companies across the entire semiconductor industrial chain from chip design, equipment, chip manufacturing, testing & packaging, and materials. The money is spread thinly between each individual company. In comparison, Intel invested $13.6 billion in R&D and spent $14.3 billion on capital expenditures in 2020.[244] The gap in R&D spending remains huge.

The Fund also has a very aggressive investment time horizon. It has a 15-year investment timeline, with a period of five years for investing, followed by five years for exits with another five years to be used as an extension. It is structured more similarly to how private equity firms plan, with a few more years of extension generously provided. A national strategic investment vehicle geared for the semiconductor sector should have aimed to provide more patient capital suitable for the industry's notoriously long cycles.

Yet, in the same policy document that called for the establishment of the Fund, the State Council set another ambitious target: to have the Chinese semiconductor supply chain reach internationally leading levels by 2030. It seems Beijing has not learned the lesson that there is no "great leap forward" in the semiconductor industry, especially not in China, where the industry is already a laggard and under strict tech restrictions.

Not to mention that China also faces a significant talent shortage in the semiconductor space, with some estimates putting the shortage at 300,000 to 400,000 professionally trained semiconductor talent as of 2020.[245] Even though private investment in China's chips sector reached a historic level, at $21.6 billion in 2020 and quadrupling from 2019, around 70 percent of the investment was in chip design. Chip design is the least capital-intensive segment within the industry, but it's not the area where the U.S. stranglehold hurts China, namely in chip manufacturing, equipment, and materials.[246]

The challenges are enormous, but there are some positive changes. The first is every Chinese company's urgent and strong motivation to ensure their own chip supplies under the Sword of Damocles of potential U.S. sanctions. Chinese corporate interests have never been more aligned with the national objective of semiconductor self-sufficiency. This will galvanize significant private sector resources, talent, and capital within the chips sector.

Another huge advantage is the scale of China's semiconductor sector. It has been the world's largest IC consuming market since 2005, and its share of the global IC market will increase. China and Asia-Pacific are forecast to increase their combined share of the worldwide IC market from 63.8 percent in 2020 to 68.1 percent in 2025. Even though 60 percent of chips consumed in China was for assembling products for export, the remaining 40 percent local demand is still significant to spur strong growth of China's local IC production market.[247]

Despite an overall talent shortage, China is attracting some top semiconductor professionals. The founder of SMIC, Richard Chang, has set up another company in China dedicated to establishing a new type of IDM suitable for the local market. Zhang Jianzhong, formerly the China general manager of American chip designer Nvidia, founded a GPU chip startup called Moore Threads in China in 2020.[248] Dr. Tang Shan, who previously worked at the U.S. chip firm Synopsys' AI Lab, helped found a chip design firm in China called Biren Tech.[249] Many other top talents like them, especially those educated overseas and worked at leading semiconductor companies, are founding startups that could help reshape China's semiconductor industry.

Overall, the Chinese semiconductor industry will remain highly vulnerable to U.S. sanctions for perhaps one decade or more. The U.S. will hold the Sword of Damocles firmly in its hands and sit in a position of strength. China will make gradual progress toward self-sufficiency in mature technologies, but even this will take much longer than Beijing has budgeted.

The U.S. is likely to keep its "hedging" strategy, allowing U.S. chip companies to sell over $100 billion worth of chips to China[250] and keep Chinese industries reliant on U.S. chips. The semiconductor sector will remain fundamentally globalized because it is simply unrealistic to have it any other way. It is estimated that to achieve fully self-sufficient localized supply chains for each region would cost the world $900 billion to $1.225 trillion in upfront investment and $45 billion to $125 billion in incremental annual operating cost, leading to a 35 to 65 percent increase in semiconductor prices.[251]

The U.S.-China chip battle and the effort by each region to bring more chip manufacturing capabilities onshore are adding great uncertainty to the global semiconductor sector. Policies from the U.S., Europe, China, South Korea, and other countries distort market dynamics and global supply chains. Migrating and creating new portions of the global chip manufacturing capabilities to the U.S. and Europe could undoubtedly lead to higher prices as transportation costs would rise and incorporate higher labor and overall costs into the entire industrial chain.

It could also lead to an oversupply of chip manufacturing capacity. As some of these foundries cost billions of U.S. dollars to build, overcapacity could mean significant financial losses if fab utilization rates fall. Suppose there is an untimely economic downturn; it could further exacerbate the situation. During the Dotcom bubble burst in 2001, the average fab utilization rates fell from 100 percent to 48 percent. TSMC saw its rate drop to 40 percent and some other foundries even lower to under 40 percent.[252] Any such scenario would indeed be an outcome where everyone loses.

Besides semiconductors, the U.S. also has other tech strangleholds on China, including operating systems, airplane engines, advanced medical equipment, and advanced materials. Washington could cause much greater harm to China's technology sector if it chooses to do so. Cutting off supplies on any of these would lead to devastating consequences within the entire Chinese tech ecosystem, and this would, in turn, disrupt the global tech sector, including damage to the U.S. markets.

For 5G and artificial intelligence, a partial decoupling is similarly unfolding between the U.S. and China. Under U.S. influence and pressure, countries representing more than 60 percent of the world's cellular equipment market are considering or have already enacted restrictions against Huawei.[253] The global infrastructure for the next generation telecommunication network is splitting into two pieces: Huawei or sans-Huawei. But because of Huawei's clout in 5G-related patents, the U.S. is allowing American companies to continue working with Huawei on setting 5G standards and supplying less advanced chips to Huawei.

In the area of AI, the U.S. is curbing Chinese investments in American technology companies, and it's keeping a more vigilant eye on AI talent flows while strengthening enforcement of technology or trade secret cases by Chinese employees at American firms. Yet, Chinese AI companies continue to rely on American chips to power their AI products. They continue to follow in the footsteps of American companies for product iterations and research direction. Chinese students are still studying AI at American universities, and collaboration between Chinese students and their American counterparts on research projects continues.

But the situation is deteriorating rapidly as the boundaries of U.S.-China tech battlegrounds expand. Data security or data sovereignty is increasingly shaping up to be the next fire zone, as evidenced by recent Chinese regulatory action against Chinese tech companies listed in the

U.S., such as ride-hailing firm Didi Global Inc. on data security grounds. It then extended to the financial market, as U.S. regulators temporarily halted IPOs of Chinese companies. [254] Such a trend is extremely concerning. The situation could quickly get out of control without the will to improve bilateral ties or work together to solve differences.

But ultimately, time is on China's side if we look at 20 to 30 years into the future. Suppose the next couple of decades are marked by "muddling through" as the two countries keep battling in some areas yet remain fundamentally integrated, then China would eventually catch up technologically and achieve increasing technological autonomy barring any unforeseen mistakes or disruptions. China's crashing scale would generate such gravitational pull that it would command a much larger market share, which could help nurture large Chinese tech companies that can eventually compete at a global scale.

Of course, making predictions that far into the future is a dangerous undertaking, especially when the uncertainties at present are already overwhelming. Both Washington and Beijing appear to behave rationally to advance their own interests. Washington needs to maintain its technological superiority and tech "nuclear weapon" against China. Beijing, of course, wants to escape the curse of the Sword of Damocles. Washington's tactics so far have worked to slow China's tech advances, but it can't push the inevitable – China's narrowing tech gap with the U.S. – indefinitely.

However, superior technological power doesn't have to be mutually exclusive. Both countries can be tech powerhouses, each with different sets of strengths and weaknesses. While the U.S. may be weaker in terms of future market scale and mass commercial application, China might lag relatively behind in fundamental research and original innovation for a very long time. These are, in fact, complementary strengths and weaknesses, where cooperation could benefit both countries - one country's yin for the other's yang.

Bilateral conditions are worsening so rapidly that effective communication, let alone cooperation, seems hard to achieve in today's environment. In recent discourse, the issue of value systems and ideology is complicating the picture. The idea of the Internet as a democratizing force has essentially been killed. China is often quoted as the prime example of "twenty-first-century authoritarianism that marries social control and efficiency."[255]

To prevent China's techno-authoritarianism from going global is an issue that unites both political parties in the U.S. "China poses perhaps the greatest threat to democracy: developing tools of oppression at home and exporting these digital technologies of repression," said Rep. Adam Schiff.[256]

But the challenges brought about by emerging new technologies such as face-recognition cameras, all-powerful data tracking, misinformation, and information manipulation are serious questions for all of us. In her exemplary book, "The Age of Surveillance Capitalism," Harvard professor Shoshana Zuboff offered a sobering description of how American high-tech giants mine and exploit private user information to undermine personal autonomy and erode democracy.[257]

China is at the other end of the spectrum where the government and tech giants work together to control and manipulate the populace. Beijing has taken stakes in its tech giants, including Bytedance, to formalize such an alliance of control.[258] However, the idea of Beijing exporting techno-authoritarianism is as sound as Washington exporting democracy via a McDonald's Happy Meal. It has not worked in either case. The reality is that technology, instead of having an inherent liberating or suppressing force, is just a tool that can be used by every ideology or authority to suit its own ends.

A global problem requires a global solution. Countries need to find ways to work together to establish globalized standards and policies to address surveillance technology, information manipulation, cyber attacks, and personal data tracking. For the U.S. and China, focusing on solving each specific problem at hand might be a more practical way forward than trying to find an all-encompassing solution to all of their differences. In trying to solve each specific problem, such as whether Tiktok should be allowed to operate in the U.S., both should adopt a cautious attitude to shrink the boundaries of the issue instead of expanding.

Of course, the U.S.-China tech "war" is only part of humanity's immense challenges as climate change, and global pandemics beat their steady drums. How these challenges interact and impact each other will likely add more uncertainty to our future.

Inside China, however, there are signs that an increasingly restrictive political environment under the leadership of Xi Jinping could stall the country's tech advance.

The technological progress made in China during the past forty years was based on gradually removing politics from science and technology endeavors. Aside from social science, political principles have not been emphasized by universities or corporates in their R&D work. Performance reviews were standardized with objective scoring metrics. Speech on non-social-science and technical topics is relatively free.

These factors, coupled with a thriving private market, led to China becoming the only non-democratic country among the top 30 countries in the Global Innovation Index during much of the 2010s,[259] challenging the long-held notion that only democratic nations can be truly innovative.

But a tightening political environment could disrupt China's technological progress from the inside. There are signs that it might be happening already. A Shanghai doctor who posted on social media that "the world will need to co-exist with the Covid virus" was being silenced and investigated for potential plagiarism in his Ph.D. thesis written decades ago. This took place after a former government official wrote on the People's Daily that the relationship between humans and viruses is one of "either one kills the other, or be killed."[260]

This is just one example where the discussion of scientific topics is becoming politicized. In addition, an increasing number of public figures have been silenced, including many whose speech had been considered "mild" before. There is not a great distance to go from here to calling the quantum theory "idealism pseudoscience" or trying to apply "criticism of idealism to physics." If China's social and political environment deteriorates to that degree, it will gut China's tech powerhouse from the inside.

The truly ironic parallel is that in 2021, science and technology (*Ke Ji*) are still viewed by China through a utilitarian lens. It is a tool for a Chinese renaissance. It is a tool for the ruling party. It is a tool to maintain control. That may be why Needham's Question won't be answered any time soon.

References

[1] Stracqualursi, Veronia. *10 times Trump attacked China and its trade relations with the US*, November 9, 2017, ABC News. https://abcnews.go.com/Politics/10-times-trump-attacked-china-trade-relations-us/story?id=46572567 Retrieved on August 2, 2021

[2] Packard, George R. *The Coming U.S.-Japan Crisis*, Foreign Affairs, vol. 66, no. 2, 1987, pp. 348–367. JSTOR, www.jstor.org/stable/20043377. Retrieved on August 3, 2021.

[3] Frankel, Jeffrey; Kahler, Miles. (1993). *Regionalism and Rivalry: Japan and the United States in Pacific Asia*, The University of Chicago Press, P. 321-390

[4] Needham, Joseph. (1969). *The Grand Titration: Science and Society in East and West*. London: Allen & Unwin, p.190–217.

[5] Sivin, Nathan. *The Needham Question*. Oxford Bibliographies, https://www.oxfordbibliographies.com/view/document/obo-9780199920082/obo-9780199920082-0006.xml Retrieved on August 4, 2021

[6] Definition is according to Oxford Languages.

[7] Definition is according to Oxford Languages.

[8] Needham, Joseph. (1969). *The Grand Titration: Science and Society in East and West*, London: Allen & Unwin, p.16-190.

[9] Merton, Robert K. (1938). *Science and the Social Order*. Philosophy of Science, p. 321–337.

[10] Wu, Wenjun, Bai, Shangshu, Li, Di, et al. (1999). *Grand Series of History of Chinese Mathematics*. Beijing Normal University Publishing Group, volume 1, p. 480.

[11] Needham, Joseph. *(1959). Science and Civilization In China.* Cambridge University Press, Volume 3, p. 24–25, p. 121.

[12] UNESCO, Buddhist Monuments in the Horyu-ji Area, https://whc.unesco.org/en/list/660/ Retrieved November 25, 2020

[13] These 6 ancient Chinese technologies that we overlook have made great contributions to world civilization. CCTV-10.

https://new.qq.com/omn/20191005/20191005A0H8R200.html Retrieved December 2, 2020

[14] Keji Xingzhe. *How snowflakes are formed has always been a mystery. This physicist wants to be a person who clears the fog*, http://www.360doc.com/content/20/1012/16/71888828_940095859.shtml Retrieved on December 3, 2020

[15] Wu Guosheng. *On whether there was science in ancient China.* http://www.kexuemag.cn/Article/ShowInfo.asp?InfoID=13637 Retrieved on December 10, 2020

[16] No consensus author. Da Xue (The Great Learning), Li Ji (The Book of Rites), written during the late Warring States (5th century-221 BCE) and Former Han periods (206 BCE-8 CE).

[17] Olerich, Rebecca. (2017). *An Examination of the Needham Question: Why Didn't China Have A Scientific Revolution Considering Its Early Scientific Accomplishments?* The City University of New York, p. 62-63.

[18] Yang, Guangxian. (1665) *Bu De Yi.*

[19] The death penalty was later lifted for some including Johann Adam Schall von Bell.

[20] Han, Qi. *Science, Knowledge, and Power: Sun Shadow Observation and Kangxi's Role in Calendar Reform*, Studies In The History of Natural Sciences, Vol. 30 No. 1 (2011). http://english.ihns.cas.cn/Publications_new/Ra/201310/W020131014609393023982.pdf Retrieved on August 4, 2021

[21] Emperor Kangxi is good at Western scientific and technological knowledge, why didn't he bring the Industrial Revolution to China? Baidu Baike. https://baike.baidu.com/tashuo/browse/content?id=3e534ed059174046fa5428f3 Retrieved on August 4, 2021

[22] Dong, Lihui. *The Western Visual Enlightenment in the Ming and Qing Dynasties*, September 11, 2019. https://www.thepaper.cn/newsDetail_forward_4344552 Retrieved on August 4, 2021

[23] Beijing Daily. *Journal of McCartney's Visit in China.* http://www.xinhuanet.com/book/2018-10/17/c_129972345_2.htm Retrieved January 10, 2021

[24] Britannica, T. Editors of Encyclopedia. *Horatio Nelson Lay. Encyclopedia Britannica.* https://www.britannica.com/biography/Horatio-Nelson-Lay Retrieved January 27, 2021

[25] Xia, Dongyuan. (1996). *History Of Westernization Movement*, p47, East China Normal University Press

[26] Wang Ermin. (1963). *The Emergence of Qing's Military Industry.* Institute of Modern History, Academia Sinica.

[27] He, Guoxiang et al. (2017). A Hundred Years History: The Origin and Growth of the Group of Chinese Sci-tech Workers, China Science Publishing & Media.

[28] Wong, William. *Oakland CA Chinatown Makes Aviation History*. San Francisco Chronicle. September 18, 2009 https://blog.sfgate.com/wwong/2009/09/18/oakland-ca-chinatown-makes-aviation-history/ Retrieved Feburary10, 2021

[29] He, Guoxiang et al. (2017). *A Hundred Years History: The Origin and Growth of the Group of Chinese Sci-tech Workers*, China Science Publishing & Media

[30] Xinhuanet. China's self-produced aircraft. China Flying Tiger Research Society. http://www.flyingtiger-cacw.com/gb_673.htm Retrieved February 19, 2021

[31] Yao, Jun. (1998). *Modern History of Aviation in China*, Elephant Press.

[32] Shihai Qihang. *The Republic of China Had Aircraft Manufacturing Plants too*. https://kknews.cc/zh-sg/history/xl4xbrg.html Retrieved on March 25, 2021

[33] Wu, Daguan. (2009). *Biography of Wu Daguan*, Aviation Industry Press

[34] Werner Ballhaus, Dr.-Ing. Alessandro Pagella, Constantin Vogel and Christoph Wilmsmeier. *Faster, greener, smarter – reaching beyond the horizon in the world of semiconductors*. PricewaterhouseCoopers AG. https://www.pwc.com/gx/en/technology/publications/assets/pwc-faster-greener-smarter.pdf Retrieved on March 28, 2020

[35] Lu, Mengjun. *In Remembrance of Chinese Semiconductor Development Pioneer Huang Chang: Work for the Country*, The Paper, June 9, 2018. https://www.thepaper.cn/newsDetail_forward_2182255 Retrieved on April 1, 2020.

[36] In 2015, the school was renamed Harvard John A. Paulson School of Engineering and Applied Sciences following a $400 million gift by Harvard Business School alumnus John A. Paulson. https://www.nytimes.com/2015/06/04/education/john-paulson-gives-400-million-to-harvard-for-engineering-school.html Retrieved on April 2, 2020

[37] Fang, Ru. *TSMC Chairman Morris Chang: Extreme Manufacturing*, Global Entrepreneurs, https://www.reuters.com/article/idCNCHINA-2895320100825 Retrieved on April 5, 2020.

[38] Southeast Television Station. https://v.ifeng.com/c/82UScmRQ5zB Retrieved on April 8, 2020.

[39] *People Who Light Up Taiwan. The Godfather of Taiwan's Semiconductors Industry: Morris Chang*. https://taiwan.k12ea.gov.tw/index.php?inter=people&id=27 Retrieved on April 10, 2020

[40] Lu, Mengjun. *In Remembrance of Chinese Semiconductor Development Pioneer Huang Chang: Work for the Country*, The Paper, June 9, 2018.

[41] Lu, Mengjun. *In Remembrance of Chinese Semiconductor Development Pioneer Huang Chang: Work for the Country*. The Paper. June 9, 2018.

[42] Wu, Xijiu. *Returning Home*, Shanghai Lexicographical Publishing House, 2012

[43] Youngblood, TIm. *Jack Kilby and the World's First Integrated Circuit, All About Circuits*, September 16, 2017, https://www.allaboutcircuits.com/news/jack-kilby-and-the-world-first-integrated-circuit/ Retrieved April 15, 2020

44 *Chinese Computer Development History*. School of Mathematical Sciences, East China Normal University.
http://math.ecnu.edu.cn/~jypan/Teaching/ParaComp/docs/HistoryChina1.html
Retrieved on April 18, 2020

45 Two Bombs, One Satellite was an early nuclear and space project of the People's Republic of China. Two Bombs refers to the atomic bomb (and later the hydrogen bomb) and the intercontinental ballistic missile (ICBM), while One Satellite refers to the artificial satellite. China tested its first atomic bomb and first hydrogen bomb in 1964 and 1967 respectively, combining the atomic bomb with surface-to-surface missile in 1966, and successfully launched its first satellite Dong Fang Hong I in 1970.

46 Suarez-Villa, Luis, and Pyo-Hwan Han. (1990). *The Rise of Korea's Electronics Industry: Technological Change, Growth, and Territorial Distribution*, Economic Geography, p. 273-92.

47 News of the Communist Party of China. *Memorabilia of the Communist Party of China, 1956* http://cpc.people.com.cn/GB/64162/64164/4416035.html *Retrieved on April 23, 2020*

48 Qiu, Songqing. *An Review of Industrial Policy in Nanjing National Government*, China Socioeconomic History Research, Vol. 4, 1998. p. 89-92

49 Sun, Yinglan. *The first plan in the history of Chinese science and technology*. Liaowang Magazine. September, 2009

50 Williams, Alex, Khan, Hassan. *A Brief History of Semiconductors: How The US Cut Costs and Lost the Leading Edge*. https://employamerica.medium.com/a-brief-history-of-semiconductors-how-the-us-cut-costs-and-lost-the-leading-edge-c21b96707cd2
Retrieved on April 23, 2020

51 Zhang, Jiuchun, Zhang, Bochun. *China's planning measures of computing technology and Soviet aid in the 1950s*. China Historical Materials of Science and Technology, Vol. 24 No. 3; 2003

52 Ye, Yonglie. (2016). *Biography of Chen Boda*. Sichuan People's Publishing House.

53 Chen Boda, Chen, Xiaonong. (2005) *Chen Boda's Final Oral Memories*. Sunshine Global Publishing Hong Kong Co., Ltd., Xingker Publishing Company.

54 *Trends in the Semiconductor Industry*, Semiconductor History Museum of Japan. https://www.shmj.or.jp/english/trends/trd80s.html Retrieved on August 4, 2021

55 *Morris Chang 2021 Speech Full Text*. April 24, 2021, EET China. https://www.eet-china.com/news/41a11361.html Retrieved on August 4, 2021

56 Morris Chang gave a speech "Cherish Taiwan's Advantages in Semiconductor Manufacturing "on April 21, 2021 in Taiwan. Video access via https://mp.weixin.qq.com/s/RsTD8AMuM0JK2ah9xpITAA Retrieved on April 26, 2021

57 Morris Chang gave a speech "Cherish Taiwan's Advantages in Semiconductor Manufacturing "on April 21, 2021 in Taiwan. Video access via https://mp.weixin.qq.com/s/RsTD8AMuM0JK2ah9xpITAA Retrieved April 27, 2020

⁵⁸ Lu, Mengjun. *Remembering Huang Chang, the leader of China's integrated circuit development: working for the country*, The Paper, June 9, 2018.
https://www.thepaper.cn/newsDetail_forward_2182255 Retrieved April 30, 2021

⁵⁹ Xiong, Wenming. *In-depth review of China's semiconductor industry, how it missed three decades of golden development*, Taihe Industry Observer, October 29, 2020.
https://finance.sina.com.cn/tech/csj/2020-10-29/doc-iiznctkc8374029.shtml Retrieved on April 30, 2021.

⁶⁰ Liu, Zhen. *Black-and-White, color, and digital televisions*, Sanlian Life Weekly, April 29, 2004. http://www.lifeweek.com.cn/2004/0429/8631.shtml Retrieved on April 30, 2021

⁶¹ China Semiconductor Industry Association. *A review and forecast of China's IC industry 30 years after the reform and opening up*, December 9, 2008.
https://www.szicc.net/MicroStation/NewsDetail.aspx?cid=6271&fid=372 Retrieved on May 6, 2021

⁶² List of semiconductor fabrication plants.
https://en.wikipedia.org/wiki/List_of_semiconductor_fabrication_plants Retrieved on May 6, 2021. This list uses channel length, which is a measure roughly equal to gate length. But there might be some slight differences, though for 250nm and above chips, the differences are negligible. The comparison therefore should be viewed as a rough contrast, but accurate calibration.

⁶³ Chen, Fang, Dong, Ruifeng. The true conditions of China's chips industry. Zhenghedao. May 25, 2019. https://www.eet-china.com/mp/a3612.html Retrieved May 10, 2021.

⁶⁴ The nm numbers should be viewed as a rough equivalent of gate length, not exact numbers as explained in footnote 53.

⁶⁵ Chen, Fang, Dong, Ruifeng. *The true conditions of China's chips industry*, Zhenghedao, May 25, 2019. https://www.eet-china.com/mp/a3612.html Retrieved on May 10, 2021.

⁶⁶ Chen, Fang, Dong, Ruifeng. *The true conditions of China's chips industry*, Zhenghedao, May 25, 2019. https://www.eet-china.com/mp/a3612.html Retrieved on May 10, 2021.

⁶⁷ Wang, Yangyuan. *The weaknesses and development strategy of China's IC industry*, Keji Daobao, May 10, 2021. https://power.in-en.com/html/power-2387477.shtml Retrieved on May 10, 2021.

⁶⁸ *Chip sales slowing. Worldwide semiconductor sales rose 31 percent in 2000, but seen slowing in 2001*, CNN.com. https://money.cnn.com/2001/01/02/technology/semi/ Retrieved on May 10, 2021.

⁶⁹ https://www.tjnj.net/searchview/xj35/DSJCL/2.html Retrieved on May 10, 2021.

⁷⁰ Li, Guojie. *Blue Book of China Computer Report*. March 10, 2011.
http://www.ict.ac.cn/liguojiewenxuan_162523/wzlj/lgjxsbg/201912/t20191227_5476685.html. Retrieved on May 10, 2021.

⁷¹ *Thirty years in China: from 1978 to 2008*, iFeng.com
http://news.ifeng.com/special/30yearsit/ Retrieved on May 12, 2021

[72] *Liu Chuanzhi: High tariffs in the 1990s led to high prices and low quality for domestic computers*, Fenghuang Caijing, March 22, 2014. https://finance.ifeng.com/a/20140322/11956224_0.shtml Retrieved on August 5, 2021.

[73] Chongkai Capital. *China IC Report*. July 22, 2019. http://finance.sina.com.cn/roll/2019-07-22/doc-ihytcerm5401615.shtml Retrieved on May 10, 2021

[74] Byun, Byung Moon. (1994) *Growth and Recent Development of the Korean Semiconductor Industry*. Asian Survey, 34(8), p. 706-720.

[75] Byun, Byung Moon. (1994) *Growth and Recent Development of the Korean Semiconductor Industry*. Asian Survey, 34(8), p. 706-720.

[76] *Thirty years in China: from 1978 to 2008*, iFeng.com. http://news.ifeng.com/special/30yearsit/ Retrieved on May 13, 2021

[77] Byun, Byung Moon. (1994) *Growth and Recent Development of the Korean Semiconductor Industry*. Asian Survey, 34(8), p. 706-720.

[78] United States General Accounting Office. *Report to the ranking minority member committee on governmental affairs*, U.S. Senate. https://www.gao.gov/assets/240/234373.pdf Retrieved on May 14, 2021

[79] These two policies were: *Notice of the State Council on Issuing Several Policies to Encourage the Development of the Software Industry and the Integrated Circuit Industry*, issued on June 24, 2000 by the State Council. http://www.gov.cn/gongbao/content/2000/content_60310.htm and *Notice of the State Council on Issuing Further Policies to Encouraging the Development of the Software Industry and the Integrated Circuit Industry*, issued on January 28, 2011 by the State Council. http://www.gov.cn/zwgk/2011-02/09/content_1800432.htm Both were retrieved on May 18, 2021

[80] The World Trade Organization. China - Value-Added Tax on Integrated Circuits https://www.wto.org/english/tratop_e/dispu_e/cases_e/ds309_e.htm Retrieved on May 18, 2021

[81] Xu Xiaotian. *To develop through innovation - the decade of rapid development of China's semiconductor industry*. China Semiconductor Industry Association. November 19, 2012. http://www.csia.net.cn/Article/ShowInfo.asp?InfoID=30379 Retrieved on May 19, 2021

[82] Xu Xiaotian. *To develop through innovation - the decade of rapid development of China's semiconductor industry*. China Semiconductor Industry Association. November 19, 2012. http://www.csia.net.cn/Article/ShowInfo.asp?InfoID=30379 Retrieved on May 19, 2021

[83] *A review of China's IC Industry during the past 30 years*. China Semiconductor Industry Association. October 31, 2008. http://www.csia.net.cn/Article/ShowInfo.asp?InfoID=3715 Retrieved on May 20, 2021

[84] *China to Fall Far Short of its "Made-in-China 2025" Goal for IC Devices*. IC Insights, May 21, 2020. https://www.icinsights.com/data/articles/documents/1261.pdf. Retrieved on May 20, 2021

[85] *The evolution of business models in a disrupted value chain.* McKinsey. 2011. https://www.mckinsey.com/~/media/mckinsey/dotcom/client_service/semiconductors/pdfs/mosc_1_business_models.ashx Retrieved on May 21, 2021

[86] Wang, Xiaoxing. *Huawei's 2010 net profit was RMB23.8 billion, company announces board structure.* Nanfang Dushibao. April 18, 2011. https://tech.qq.com/a/20110418/000044.htm Retrieved on May 21, 2021

[87] *TSMC 2010 Business Overview.* https://investor.tsmc.com/static/annualReports/2010_Business_Overview_E.pdf Retrieved on May 21, 2021

[88] *The evolution of business models in a disrupted value chain.* McKinsey. 2011. https://www.mckinsey.com/~/media/mckinsey/dotcom/client_service/semiconductors/pdfs/mosc_1_business_models.ashx Retrieved on May 21, 2021

[89] *A review of China's IC design industry during the past 10 years.* China Semiconductor Industry Association. November 22, 2012. http://www.csia.net.cn/Article/ShowInfo.asp?InfoID=30419 Retrieved on May 20, 2021

[90] Xu Xiaotian. *To develop through innovation - the decade of rapid development of China's semiconductor industry.* China Semiconductor Industry Association. November 19, 2012. http://www.csia.net.cn/Article/ShowInfo.asp?InfoID=30379 Retrieved on May 20, 2021

[91] *Top answer to the Quora question: "United States is pressuring the Netherlands to block the sale of EUV equipment to SMIC by Dutch company ASML is ultimately affecting China's dream in technology".* How long US can resist China's development? https://www.quora.com/United-States-is-pressuring-the-Netherlands-to-block-the-sale-of-EUV-equipment-to-SMIC-by-Dutch-company-ASML-is-ultimately-affecting-Chinas-dream-in-technology-How-long-US-can-resist-Chinas-development Retrieved on July 26, 2021

[92] Curley, Robert. (2011) *Architects of the Information Age*, Rosen Education Service, p. 67

[93] *Xilinx and Altera no longer largest fabless chip firms.* https://www.eetimes.com/xilinx-and-altera-no-longer-largest-fabless-chip-firms/ Retrieved on June 23, 2021

[94] *TSMC First Taiwan Company to List on NYSE.* https://pr.tsmc.com/schinese/news/2085 Retrieved on June 23, 2021

[95] *How did Wuxi Huajing became Huarun Shanghua?* https://www.laoyaoba.com/html/share/news?source=app_android_v2&news_id=727395 Retrieved on June 24, 2021.

[96] *How did Wuxi Huajing became Huarun Shanghua?* https://www.laoyaoba.com/html/share/news?source=app_android_v2&news_id=727395 Retrieved on June 24, 2021.

[97] Lu, Mengjun. *Interview with Richard Chang: From SMIC to SiEn (QingDao) Integrated Circuits, he has been a serial entrepreneur.* The Paper. June 5, 2019. https://www.thepaper.cn/newsDetail_forward_3598844 Retrieved on June 24, 2021.

[99] Lu, Mengjun. *Interview with Richard Chang: From SMIC to SiEn (QingDao) Integrated Circuits, he has been a serial entrepreneur.* The Paper, June 5, 2019. https://www.thepaper.cn/newsDetail_forward_3598844 Retrieved on June 24, 2021

[100] *SMIC IPO prospectus.* https://www.sec.gov/Archives/edgar/data/1267482/000119312504040655/d424b4.htm Retrieved on June 24, 2021

[101] *SMIC internal upheaval as Datang Holdings attempts to take control.* Caixin. https://finance.qq.com/a/20110718/000209_1.htm Retrieved on June 24, 2021

[102] *SMIC IPO prospectus.* https://www.sec.gov/Archives/edgar/data/1267482/000119312504040655/d424b4.htm Retrieved on June 24, 2021

[103] *SMIC IPO prospectus.* https://www.sec.gov/Archives/edgar/data/1267482/000119312504040655/d424b4.htm Retrieved on June 24, 2021

[104] *SMIC 2004/2005 annual report to the Hong Kong Stock Exchange.* https://www.smics.com/uploads/financialchn/2011012111544017_tc.pdf https://www.smics.com/uploads/financialchn/2011012018070017_tc.pdf Retrieved on June 25, 2021

[105] *SMIC annual report 2006 to the Hong Kong Stock Exchange.* https://www.smics.com/uploads/financialchn/2011012015151217_tc.pdf Retrieved on June 25, 2021

[106] *SMIC 2006 annual report to the Hong Kong Stock Exchange.* https://www.smics.com/uploads/financialchn/2011012015151217_tc.pdf Retrieved on June 25, 2021

[107] Clendenin, Mike. *Analysis: background on TSMC, SMIC lawsuit.* EETimes. January 5, 2004. https://www.eetimes.com/analysis-background-on-tsmc-smic-lawsuit/ Retrieved on June 30, 2021

[108] Clendenin, Mike. *Analysis: background on TSMC, SMIC lawsuit.* EETimes. January 5, 2004. https://www.eetimes.com/analysis-background-on-tsmc-smic-lawsuit/ Retrieved on June 30, 2021

[109] Jiao, Jiying. *Richard Chang fined again for 10 million new Taiwan dollar; Taiwan could issue arrest warrant.* Xin Jing Bao. October 25, 2005. http://tech.sina.com.cn/it/2005-10-25/0811747259.shtml Retrieved on June 30, 2021

[110] TSMC also sued SMIC in other courts listed here.

[111] *TSMC Reaches Settlement with SMIC.* https://pr.tsmc.com/english/news/1323 Retrieved on June 30, 2021

[112] Chip maker SMIC falls on debut. CNN, http://edition.cnn.com/2004/BUSINESS/03/18/china.smic/index.html Retrieved on June 30, 2021

[113] *SMIC annual report 2006.* https://www.smics.com/uploads/financialchn/2011012015151217_tc.pdf Retrieved on July 1, 2021

[114] TSMC official website:
https://www.tsmc.com/english/dedicatedFoundry/technology/logic/l_65nm Retrieved on July 1, 2021

[115] *SMIC annual report 2006.*
https://www.smics.com/uploads/financialchn/2011012015151217_tc.pdf Retrieved on July 1, 2021

[116] *SMIC annual report 2006.*
https://www.smics.com/uploads/financialchn/2011012015151217_tc.pdf Retrieved on July 1, 2021

[117] *TSMC v. SMIC Trial. Courtroom Connect,* https://cvn.com/proceedings/tsmc-north-america-vs-semiconductor-manufacturing-international-trial-2009-09-08 Retrieved on July 1, 2021.

[118] Keating, Gina. *California jury finds SMIC stole trade secrets.* Reuters. November 3, 2009. https://www.reuters.com/article/us-smic-lawsuit-idUSTRE5A26CA20091103 Retrieved on July 2, 2021.

[119] *SMIC sues TSMC in Beijing.* Financial Times Chinese.
https://www.ftchinese.com/story/001007980?archive Retrieved on July 2, 2021

[120] *SMIC annual report 2007.*
https://www.smics.com/uploads/financialchn/2011011912304217_tc.pdf Retrieved on July 2, 2021

[121] *The case of SMIC vs. TSMC on unfair competition and commercial slander.* Chinacourt.gov. http://bjgy.chinacourt.gov.cn/paper/detail/2009/09/id/78007.shtml Retrieved on July 2, 2021

[122] *TSMC v. SMIC Trial.* Courtroom Connect, https://cvn.com/proceedings/tsmc-north-america-vs-semiconductor-manufacturing-international-trial-2009-09-08 Retrieved on July 6, 2021.

[123] *SMIC former CEO Richard Chang: My resignation is good for the company.* Netease Technology. November 11, 2009.
https://www.163.com/tech/article/5NQQD2SD000915BD.html Retrieved on July 6, 2021

[124] *My fab is bigger than yours.* The Economist. January 15, 2005.
https://www.economist.com/special-report/2005/01/15/my-fab-is-bigger-than-yours Retrieved on July 6, 2021

[125] *Global semiconductor sales fell by 2.8 percent in 2008.* Semiconductor Industry Association. February 2, 2009. https://www.semiconductors.org/global-semiconductor-sales-fell-by-2-8-percent-in-2008/ Retrieved on July 6, 2021

[126] *SMIC annual report 2008.*

[127] *SMIC internal control battles: how to keep balance in the future?* OFweek.
https://mp.ofweek.com/ee/a745683222336 Retrieved on July 7, 2021

[128] Tenorio, Nerilyn. Kwok, Donny. *China's SMIC shares surge on Datang Tel stake sale.* November 11, 2008. https://www.reuters.com/article/sppage024-hkg164490-oisnr/chinas-smic-shares-surge-on-datang-tel-stake-sale-idUSHKG16449020081111 Retrieved on July 6, 2021

[129] *SMIC internal control battles: how to keep balance in the future?* OFweek. https://mp.ofweek.com/ee/a745683222336 Retrieved on July 7, 2021

[130] *SMIC internal control battles: how to keep balance in the future?* OFweek. https://mp.ofweek.com/ee/a745683222336 Retrieved on July 7, 2021

[131] *SMIC annual report 2011.* https://www.smics.com/uploads/pdf_en/pdfs/20120425170201001414586_en.pdf and https://interfax.com/newsroom/top-stories/63233/ Retrieved on July 7, 2021

[132] Huang, Jie. *SMIC internal auditing file exposed: COO Yang Shining suspected of tax evasion.* July 08, 2011 http://roll.sohu.com/20110708/n312818445.shtml Retrieved on July 8, 2021

[133] *Fortune 500 China* https://www.fortunechina.com/china500/276/2020 Retrieved on July 9, 2021

[134] *SMIC's annual report 2012 & 2017*

[135] *SMIC historical R&D spending.* Hanghangcha. https://www.hanghangcha.com/cms/detail/224238.html Retrieved on July 9, 2021

[136] *SMIC's 15 year development.* Yunfeng Jinrong Wechat Account. https://moore.live/news/93346/detail/ Retrieved on July 9, 2021

[137] *TSMC annual reports and TSMC's official website.*

[138] Jiang, Siying. *The behind-the-scene heroes of Taiwan's semiconductor industry.* June 14, 2020. https://zhuanlan.zhihu.com/p/148228388 Retrieved on July 19, 2021

[139] Andrew F. Diamond. *Dueling Over Dual-Use Goods: The U.S. Department of Commerce's Misguided Attempt to Promote U.S. Security and Trade with China through Restrictive Export Controls.* Brooklyn Journal of Corporate, Financial & Commercial Law, 2008.

[140] The 42 countries are: Argentina, Australia, Austria, Belgium, Bulgaria, Canada, Croatia, Czech Republic, Denmark, Estonia, Finland, France, Germany, Greece, Hungary, India, Ireland, Italy, Japan, Latvia, Lithuania, Luxembourg, Malta, Mexico, Netherlands, New Zealand, Norway, Poland, Portugal, Republic of Korea, Romania, Russian Federation, Slovakia, Slovenia, Spain, South Africa, Sweden, Switzerland, Turkey, Ukraine, United Kingdom and United States.

[141] Hirsh, Michael. *The Great Technology Giveaway? Trading with Potential Foes*, Foreign Affairs, Vol. 77, No. 5, 1998.

[142] Fukuyama, Francis. (1992) *The End of History and the Last Man.* New York: Free Press.

[143] Friedman, Thomas L. (2007). *The World Is Flat.* Penguin Books.

[144] Diamond, Andrew F. *Dueling Over Dual-Use Goods: The U.S. Department of Commerce's Misguided Attempt to Promote U.S. Security and Trade with China through Restrictive Export Controls.* Brooklyn Journal of Corporate, Financial & Commercial Law, 2008.

[145] Hirsh, Michael. *The Great Technology Giveaway? Trading with Potential Foes*, Foreign Affairs, Vol. 77, No. 5, 1998.

References

[146] Diamond, Andrew F. *Dueling Over Dual-Use Goods: The U.S. Department of Commerce's Misguided Attempt to Promote U.S. Security and Trade with China through Restrictive Export Controls*. Brooklyn Journal of Corporate, Financial & Commercial Law, 2008.

[147] Godsey, Matthew, Milhollin, Gary. *In China We Trust? Lowering U.S. Controls on Militarily Useful Exports to China*. The Wisconsin Project on Nuclear Arms Control. https://www.wisconsinproject.org/in-china-we-trust-lowering-u-s-controls-on-militarily-useful-exports-to-china/ Retrieved on July 21, 2021

[148] Diamond, Andrew F. *Dueling Over Dual-Use Goods: The U.S. Department of Commerce's Misguided Attempt to Promote U.S. Security and Trade with China through Restrictive Export Controls*. Brooklyn Journal of Corporate, Financial & Commercial Law, 2008.

[149] Hirsh, Michael. *The Great Technology Giveaway? Trading with Potential Foes*, Foreign Affairs, Vol. 77, No. 5, 1998

[150] *Export Controls: Rapid Advances in China's Semiconductor Industry Underscore Need for Fundamental U.S. Policy Review* (19-APR-2002, GAO-02-620). https://www.govinfo.gov/content/pkg/GAOREPORTS-GAO-02-620/html/GAOREPORTS-GAO-02-620.htm Retrieved on July 27, 2021.

[151] *2020 Year-end Sanctions and Export Controls Update*. Gibson Dunn, February 5, 2021. https://www.gibsondunn.com/wp-content/uploads/2021/02/2020-year-end-sanctions-and-export-controls-update.pdf Retrieved on July 22, 2021

[152] Viswanatha, Aruna; Dou, Eva; O'Keeffe, Kate. *ZTE to Pay $892 Million to U.S., Plead Guilty in Iran Sanctions Probe*, March 7, 2017. https://www.wsj.com/articles/zte-to-pay-892-million-to-u-s-plead-guilty-in-iran-sanctions-probe-1488902019 Retrieved on July 22, 2021

[153] Xinpiange. *Can China reach 70 self-sufficiency rate in 2025?* May 1, 2021. https://www.eet-china.com/mp/a48834.html Retrieved on July 22, 2021.

[154] *China to Fall Far Short of its "Made-in-China 2025" Goal for IC Devices*, IC Insights, May 21, 2020. https://www.icinsights.com/news/bulletins/China-To-Fall-Far-Short-Of-Its-MadeinChina-2025-Goal-For-IC-Devices/ Retrieved on July 22, 2021.

[155] *The signature of Liang Mengsong*, Wechat account Caijwj. December 20, 2020. https://www.pingwest.com/a/226897 Retrieved on July 22, 2021.

[156] Xiang, Chenzhen; Hong, Youfang. *Executive quit and joins Samsung with secrets, TSMC wins lawsuit but loses advantages,* August 25, 2015. https://ec.ltn.com.tw/article/paper/909702 Retrieved on July 22, 2021.

[157] Chen, Rongliang. *Hunting for rebels: revealing the story of Liang Mengsong's contribution to Samsung*, Common Wealth Magazine, January 20, 2015. https://www.cw.com.tw/article/5063951?template=transformers Retrieved on July 23, 2021.

[158] *Liang Mengsong's career destiny*. Finance Times, December 15, 2020. https://www.zvstus.com/article/news/1/a2897ffffe8993f466683f3e47410000.html Retrieved on July 23, 2021.

[159] *The signature of Liang Mengsong,* Wechat account Caijwj, December 20, 2020. https://www.pingwest.com/a/226897 Retrieved on July 22, 2021.

[160] *TSMC sues Liang Mengsong for leaking secrets, and the Supreme Court sentenced Samsung to be banned from office before the end of 2015*, Taiwan International Patent & Law Office, September 2015. https://www.tiplo.com.tw/tw/tn_in.aspx?mnuid=1242&nid=45721 Retrieved on July 26, 2021.

[161] Chen, Rongliang. *Hunting for rebels: revealing the story of Liang Mengsong's contribution to Samsung*, Common Wealth Magazine, January 20, 2015. https://www.cw.com.tw/article/5063951?template=transformers Retrieved on July 26, 2021.

[162] Chen, Rongliang. *Hunting for rebels: revealing the story of Liang Mengsong's contribution to Samsung*, Common Wealth Magazine, January 20, 2015. https://www.cw.com.tw/article/5063951?template=transformers Retrieved on July 26, 2021.

[163] Chen, Rongliang. *Hunting for rebels: revealing the story of Liang Mengsong's contribution to Samsun,* Common Wealth Magazine, January 20, 2015.

[164] *The signature of Liang Mengsong.* Wechat account Caijwj, December 20, 2020. https://www.pingwest.com/a/226897 Retrieved on July 26, 2021

[165] There are doubts about SMIC's claim of its 95 percent high yield rate as industry experts question whether the company have the ability to achieve it. The doubts continue until today. See also: *SMIC Rumored To Have Achieved 95% 14nm Chip Yield – But Industry Insiders Doubt The Claim* https://wccftech.com/smic-rumored-to-have-achieved-95-14nm-chip-yield-but-industry-insiders-doubt-the-claim/ Retrieved on July 26, 2017. But the point here about Liang helping SMIC to advance technologically still stands despite this particularly doubt.

[166] *Chinese Military Companies Sanctions.* U.S. Department of the Treasury. https://home.treasury.gov/policy-issues/financial-sanctions/sanctions-programs-and-country-information/chinese-military-companies-sanctions Retrieved on July 26, 2021

[167] Nellis, Stephen. *ASML extends sales deal with Chinese chipmaker SMIC to end of 2021,* March 3, 2021. https://www.reuters.com/article/us-asml-holding-smic-idUSKBN2AV1S6 Retrieved on July 26, 2021.

[168] *SMIC reportedly gets US license to import mature process equipment.* Global Times, March 2, 2021. https://www.globaltimes.cn/page/202103/1216999.shtml Retrieved on July 27, 2021.

[169] Strumpf, Dan. *U.S. Weighs Export Controls on China's Top Chip Maker,* Wall Street Journal, September 6, 2020. https://www.wsj.com/articles/u-s-weighs-export-controls-on-chinas-top-chip-maker-11599324489 Retrieved on July 26, 2021.

[170] Edited Transcript of 0981.HK earnings conference call or presentation 5-Feb-21. https://money.yahoo.com/edited-transcript-0981-hk-earnings-003000612.html Retrieved on July 27, 2021

References

---

[171] *Export Controls: Rapid Advances in China's Semiconductor Industry Underscore Need for Fundamental U.S. Policy Review* (19-APR-2002,GAO-02-620). https://www.govinfo.gov/content/pkg/GAOREPORTS-GAO-02-620/html/GAOREPORTS-GAO-02-620.htm Retrieved on July 27, 2021.

[172] ASIC is Application-Specific Integrated Circuit.

[173] *From 0 to 50 billion: Huawei's 28-year history of making chips*, Zhidongxi. https://tech.sina.cn/csj/2019-06-17/doc-ihvhiqay6160648.d.html?wm=4007 Retrieved on May 25, 2021

[174] It is unclear which EDA software Huawei purchase initially, but as of 2019, Huawei used EDA software from Synopsys, Cadence, and Mentor Graphics, all American companies and industry leaders.

[175] R&D intensity is generally defined as expenditures by a firm on its research and development divided by the firm's sales.

[176] Yin, Zhixin, Yuan, Like, Li Zhenxing. *Global Innovation Layout and Model Selection of High-tech Enterprises - A Case Study on Huawei,* China Academic Journal Electronic Publishing House, October 2017. file:///Users/jixiang/Desktop/%E9%AB%98%E7%A7%91%E6%8A%80%E4%BC%81%E4%B8%9A%E5%85%A8%E7%90%83%E5%88%9B%E6%96%B0%E5%B8%83%E5%B1%80%E5%8F%8A%E6%A8%A1%E5%BC%8F%E9%80%89%E6%8B%A9_%E4%BB%A5%E5%8D%8E%E4%B8%BA%E5%85%AC%E5%8F%B8%E4%B8%BA%E4%BE%8B_%E5%B0%B9%E5%BF%97%E6%AC%A3.pdf.pdf Retrieved on June 7, 2021

[177] *China R&D Expenditure Report 2020*, Dalian University of Technology. May 6, 2021. http://m.zhishifenzi.com/news/multiple/11239.html Retrieved on June 7, 2021

[178] *Report on China R&D Expenditure*, DUT School of Economics and Management, https://www.sciping.com/wp-content/uploads/2019/05/%E4%B8%AD%E5%9B%BD%E7%A0%94%E5%8F%91%E7%BB%8F%E8%B4%B9%E6%8A%A5%E5%91%8A%EF%BC%882018%EF%BC%89.pdf Retrieved on July 28, 2021

[179] Skillicorn, Nick. *Top 1000 companies that spend the most on Research & Development (charts and analysis)*, Ideastovalue, August 28, 2019. https://www.ideatovalue.com/inno/nickskillicorn/2019/08/top-1000-companies-that-spend-the-most-on-research-development-charts-and-analysis/ Retrieved on June 7, 2021

[180] *From 0 to 50 billion: Huawei's 28-year history of making chips*, Zhidongxi. https://tech.sina.cn/csj/2019-06-17/doc-ihvhiqay6160648.d.html?wm=4007 Retrieved on June 4, 2021

[181] *From 0 to 50 billion: Huawei's 28-year history of making chips*, Zhidongxi. https://tech.sina.cn/csj/2019-06-17/doc-ihvhiqay6160648.d.html?wm=4007 Retrieved on May 25, 2021

[182] Huawei Technologies. *Huawei reports record revenues*, January 18, 2004. https://www.itweb.co.za/content/j5alr7Qll4LvpYQk Retrieved on may 25, 2021

[183] Yin, Zhixin, Yuan, Like, Li Zhenxing. *Global Innovation Layout and Model Selection of High-tech Enterprises - A Case Study on Huawei*, China Academic Journal Electronic Publishing House, October 2017. file:///Users/jixiang/Desktop/%E9%AB%98%E7%A7%91%E6%8A%80%E4%BC%81%E4%B8%9A%E5%85%A8%E7%90%83%E5%88%9B%E6%96%B0%E5%B8%83%E5%B1%80%E5%8F%8A%E6%A8%A1%E5%BC%8F%E9%80%89%E6%8B%A9_%E4%BB%A5%E5%8D%8E%E4%B8%BA%E5%85%AC%E5%8F%B8%E4%B8%BA%E4%BE%8B_%E5%B0%B9%E5%BF%97%E6%AC%A3.pdf.pdf Retrieved on June 8, 2021

[184] Lian, Yuhui. *Big HiSilicon turning left, Small HiSilicon turning right? The misunderstandings of the public for Huawei chips and its potential impact*, EqualOcean, January 5, 2020. https://www.iyiou.com/analysis/20200105121584 Retrieved on June 7, 2021

[185] Kharpal, Arjun. *Huawei is "open" to selling 5G chips to Apple for iPhones, marking a big shift in strategy*, CNBC.com. https://www.cnbc.com/2019/04/15/huawei-is-open-to-selling-5g-chips-to-apple-for-iphones.html Retrieved on June 8, 2021

[186] Huawei Technologies. *Huawei reports record revenues*, January 18, 2004. https://www.itweb.co.za/content/j5alr7Qll4LvpYQk Retrieved on may 26, 2021

[187] Dai, Hui. *How did Huawei HiSilicon's Kirin chip emerge?* https://zhuanlan.zhihu.com/p/45707743 Retrieved on May 26, 2021

[188] Dai, Hui. *How did Huawei HiSilicon's Kirin chip emerge?* https://zhuanlan.zhihu.com/p/45707743 Retrieved on May 26, 2021

[189] Xiao, Jian. *Domestic made quad-core CPUs show off: A review of Huawei D1 quad-core XL mobile phone*, October 10, 2012. http://tech.sina.com.cn/mobile/n/2012-10-10/15387688746.shtml Retrieved on May 27, 2021

[190] Dai, Hui. *How did Huawei HiSilicon's Kirin chip emerge?* https://zhuanlan.zhihu.com/p/45707743 Retrieved on May 26, 2021

[191] Li, Na. *Huawei's device unit aims for 100 million unit in sales this year, to establish in the European market in three years*, Diyi Caijing Daily, May 9, 2014. https://it.sohu.com/20140509/n399333801.shtml Retrieved on June 1, 2021

[192] *HiSilicon Kirin 925 vs Qualcomm Snapdragon 652*, https://versus.com/en/hisilicon-kirin-925-vs-qualcomm-snapdragon-652 Retrieved on June 8, 2021

[193] *A review of the development of high-end Kirin chips*, https://xw.qq.com/cmsid/20200902A03EO900 Retrieved on June 10, 201

[194] *HiSilicon Kirin 950 vs Qualcomm Snapdragon 810 MSM8994*, https://versus.com/en/hisilicon-kirin-950-vs-qualcomm-snapdragon-810-msm8994 Retrieved on June 10, 2020

[195] *HiSilicon Kirin 950 vs Qualcomm Snapdragon 810 MSM8994*, https://versus.com/en/hisilicon-kirin-950-vs-qualcomm-snapdragon-810-msm8994 Retrieved on June 10, 2020

[196] Huawei University, Ding, Wei; Chen, Haiyan. (2019) *Entropy reduction: the source of Huawei's vitality*, CITIC Publishing Group.

References

[197] *TSMC official website* https://www.tsmc.com/english/dedicatedFoundry/technology/logic/l_16_12nm Retrieved on June 14, 2021. The website does not name HiSilicon as the company adopting 16nm FinFET process but the timeline matches with Huawei's production schedule.

[198] Huawei University, Ding, Wei; Chen, Haiyan. (2019) *Entropy reduction: the source of Huawei's vitality*, CITIC Publishing Group.

[199] *China-Based HiSilicon's Time in the Top-10 Ranking May be Short Lived*, IC Insights. https://www.icinsights.com/data/articles/documents/1286.pdf Retrieved on June 22, 2021

[200] *Revenue of Top 10 IC Design (Fabless) Companies for 2020 Undergoes 26.4% Increase YoY Due to High Demand for Notebooks and Networking Products, Says TrendForce*, https://www.trendforce.com/presscenter/news/20210325-10735.html Retrieved on June 22, 2021.

[201] *Huawei HiSilicon ranked 1st in Q1 2020 China smartphone SOC ranking*, https://www.huaweiupdate.com/huawei-hisilicon-ranked-1st-in-q1-2020-china-smartphone-soc-ranking/ Retrieved on June 22, 2021.

[202] *HiSilicon chips to power nearly 70% of Huawei handset shipments in 2019, says Digitimes Research*, https://www.digitimes.com/news/a20191024PD210.html?chid=2&mod=3&q=hisilicon Retrieved on June 22, 2021.

[203] *Huawei takes top spot in global phone shipments for first time*, BBC. https://www.bbc.com/news/technology-53594435 Retrieved on June 22, 2021.

[204] *Huawei Hisilicon Quietly Powering Tens of Millions of Western IoT Devices*, IPVM.com, December 12, 2018. https://ipvm.com/reports/huawei-hisilicon Retrieved on July 28, 2021.

[205] *Strategy Analytics: Q1 2020 Cellular Baseband Market Share: 5G Fuels Baseband Revenue Growth*, BusinessWire, June 25, 2020. https://www.businesswire.com/news/home/20200625005088/en/Strategy-Analytics-Q1-2020-Cellular-Baseband-Market-Share-5G-Fuels-Baseband-Revenue-Growth Retrieved on July 28, 2021.

[206] Jhonsa, Eric. *Qualcomm Soars After Strong Earnings and Chip Disclosures: 6 Key Takeaways*, TheStreet.com, November 4, 2020. https://www.thestreet.com/investing/qualcomm-soars-after-strong-earnings-and-chip-disclosures-6-key-takeaways Retrieved on July 28, 2021

[207] *Addition of Entities to the Entity List*, https://www.federalregister.gov/documents/2019/05/21/2019-10616/addition-of-entities-to-the-entity-list Retrieved on June 23, 2021.

[208] Patterson, Alan. *TSMC to keep supplying to Huawei*, EETimes. https://www.eetimes.com/tsmc-to-keep-supplying-chips-to-huawei/ Retrieved on June 23, 2021.

209 Wang, Lisa. *TSMC to continue supplying Huawei*, Taipei Times, May 24, 2019. https://www.taipeitimes.com/News/biz/archives/2019/05/24/2003715676 Retrieved on July 28, 2021

210 Patterson, Alan. *Huawei Catches a Break with TSMC*, EET Asia, May 28, 2019. https://www.eetasia.com/huawei-catches-a-break-with-tsmc/ Retrieved on July 28, 2021.

211 Yao, Xinlu. *The most difficult 2019 saw revenue up 19%. Huawei: 2020 will be harder; try to survive*, Quantianhou Technology, March 31, 2020. https://awtmt.com/articles/3588871 Retrieved on July 29, 2021.

212 Li, Lauly; Cheng, Ting-Fang. *Huawei builds up 2-year reserve of 'most important' US chips*, Nikkei Asia, May 28, 2020. https://asia.nikkei.com/Spotlight/Huawei-crackdown/Huawei-builds-up-2-year-reserve-of-most-important-US-chips Retrieved on July 28, 2021.

213 *Summary of the NCSC analysis of May 2020 US sanction.* National Cyber Security Center, July 14, 2020. https://www.ncsc.gov.uk/report/summary-of-ncsc-analysis-of-us-may-2020-sanction Retrieved on July 29, 2021.

214 *Ren Zhengfei: American politicians want us to die, but desire for survival makes us fight*, Beijing News, August 29, 2020. https://www.bjnews.com.cn/detail/159871157715682.html Retrieved on July 29, 2021.

215 Sui, Linda. Global Smartphone Shipments Surge to 340 Million units, Up +24% YoY in Q1 2021, StrategyAnalytics, April 19, 2021. https://www.strategyanalytics.com/strategy-analytics/blogs/devices/smartphones/smart-phones/2021/04/19/global-smartphone-shipments-surge-to-340-million-units-up-24-yoy-in-q1-2021 Retrieved on July 29, 2021.

216 *Domestic mobile phone sales ranking in May: OPPO once again ranked first, Huawei has fallen to fifth*, Cailiao, July 3, 2021. https://www.sohu.com/a/475285923_120553120 Retrieved on July 29, 2021.

217 Yamada, Shuhei. *Huawei persists in developing cutting-edge semiconductors*, Nikkei Asia, June 12, 2021. https://asia.nikkei.com/Spotlight/Comment/Huawei-persists-in-developing-cutting-edge-semiconductors Retrieved on July 29, 2021.

218 *About Huawei HiSilicon, this article is worth reading*. Semiinsights.com, May 30, 2018. https://www.sohu.com/a/233384801_132567 Retrieved on August 9, 2021.

219 *Huawei to keep HiSilicon team at all costs, continue developing Kirin processors*, Zhongguancun Online, June 14, 2021. https://www.163.com/dy/article/GCFNRRPH051189P5.html Retrieved on July 29, 2021.

220 *Huawei Hubble invests in 40 chip companies in three years: what does it want to do?* Caijing New Media, July 1, 2021. https://finance.sina.com.cn/chanjing/gsnews/2021-07-01/doc-ikqcfnca4405499.shtml Retrieved on July 30, 2021.

221 Hille, Kathrin; Yang, Yuan; Liu, Qianer. *Huawei develops plan for chip plant to help beat US sanctions*, Financial Times, October 31, 2020. https://www.ft.com/content/84eb666e-0af3-48eb-8b60-3f53b19435cb Retrieved on July 29, 2021.

[222] *Huawei Hubble invests in 40 chip companies in three years: what does it want to do?* Caijing New Media, July 1, 2021. https://finance.sina.com.cn/chanjing/gsnews/2021-07-01/doc-ikqcfnca4405499.shtml Retrieved on July 30, 2021.

[223] Ball, Jonny. *What's really behind the US's Huawei ban?* NewStatesman, November 1, 2019. https://www.newstatesman.com/spotlight-america/cyber/2019/11/whats-really-behind-uss-huawei-ban Retrieved on July 29, 2021.

[224] Duan, Lian. *Huawei P50 unveiled after four months delay: starting at RMB4,488 without 5G, can Harmony OS with 40 million users be the turning point?* Daily Economic News, July 30, 2021. http://www.nbd.com.cn/articles/2021-07-30/1858453.html Retrieved on July 30, 2021.

[225] Weber, Max. (1922). *Gesammelte Aufsatze zur Wissenschaftslehre*, Tubingen, J.C.B. Mohr, p. 213, P.A. Sorokin, Social and Cultural Dynamics, New York, American Book Co., 1937, esp. II, Chap. 2.

[226] Merton, Robert K. *Science and the Social Order*, Philosophy of Science, vol. 5, no. 3, 1938, p. 321–337. JSTOR, www.jstor.org/stable/184838. Retrieved on August 10, 2021.

[227] Yang, Jie; Yang, Stephanie; Fitch, Asa. *The World Relies on One Chip Maker in Taiwan, Leaving Everyone Vulnerable*, The Wall Street Journal, June 19, 2021. https://www.wsj.com/articles/the-world-relies-on-one-chip-maker-in-taiwan-leaving-everyone-vulnerable-11624075400 Retrieved on August 9, 2021.

[228] Franck, Thomas. *Senate passes $250 billion bipartisan tech and manufacturing bill aimed at countering China*, June 8, 2021. https://www.cnbc.com/2021/06/08/senate-passes-bipartisan-tech-and-manufacturing-bill-aimed-at-china.html, Retrieved on August 9, 2021.

[229] Vincent, James. *EU aims to double chip manufacturing amid growing fears about "digital sovereignty"*, The Verge, March 10, 2021. https://www.theverge.com/2021/3/10/22322860/eu-semiconductor-chip-supply-double-output-2030-global-compass-investment Retrieved on August 9, 2021.

[230] Qian, Tongxin. *Good for semiconductors, China's IDM model may have new opportunities*, Diyi Caijing, August 6, 2020. https://www.yicai.com/news/100725928.html Retrieved on August 18, 2021.

[231] Leonard, Jenny; Sink, Justin. *Biden Says China Won't Be Most Powerful Country on His Watch*, Bloomberg, March 25, 2021. https://www.bloomberg.com/news/articles/2021-03-25/biden-says-china-won-t-be-most-powerful-country-on-his-watch Retrieved on August 19, 2021.

[232] Franck, Thomas. *Senate passes $250 billion bipartisan tech and manufacturing bill aimed at countering China*, CNBC.com, June 8, 2021. https://www.cnbc.com/2021/06/08/senate-passes-bipartisan-tech-and-manufacturing-bill-aimed-at-china.html Retrieved on August 19, 2021.

[233] VerWey, John. *Chinese Semiconductor Industrial Policy: Prospects for Future Success*, Journal of International Commerce and Economics, August 2019. https://www.usitc.gov/publications/332/journals/chinese_semiconductor_industrial_policy_prospects_for_success_jice_aug_2019.pdf Retrieved on August 10, 2021.

[234] Ip, Greg. *"Industrial Policy" Is Back: The West Dusts Off Old Idea to Counter China*, July 29, 2021. https://www.wsj.com/articles/subsidies-chips-china-state-aid-biden-11627565906 Retrieved on August 9, 2021.

[235] Byung-yeul, Baek. *Korea to create world's largest chip manufacturing complex*, The Korean Times, May 2021. https://www.koreatimes.co.kr/www/tech/2021/05/133_308778.html Retrieved on August 10, 2021.

[236] Yap, Chuin-Wei. *State Support Helped Fuel Huawei's Global Rise*, The Wall Street Journal, December 25, 2019. https://www.wsj.com/articles/state-support-helped-fuel-huaweis-global-rise-11577280736 Retrieved on August 10, 2021.

[237] *Mapping Business Innovation Support (MABIS)Project partly funded under the Horizon 2020 Programme of the European Commission*, OECD. https://www.oecd.org/sti/rd-tax-stats-database.pdf, Retrieved on August 10, 2021.

[238] Wu, Yiyun; Zhu, Xiwei. *The determinants and effectiveness of industrial policy in China: A study based on Five-Year Plans*, China Economic Review, Volume 53, February 2019, p. 225-242.

[239] Barwick, Panle Jia; Kalouptsidi, Myrto; Zahur, Nahim Bin. *Industrial policy: lessons from China*, VOX, CEPR Policy Portal. https://voxeu.org/print/64564 Retrieved on August 19, 2021.

[240] Jongwanich, Juthathip. *Effectiveness of Industrial Policy on Firms' Productivity: Evidence from Thai Manufacturing*, ERIA Discussion Paper Series. https://www.eria.org/uploads/media/discussion-papers/Effectiveness-of-Industrial-Policy-on-Firms%E2%80%99-Productivity%3A-Evidence-from-Thai-Manufacturing.pdf Retrieved on August 19, 2021.

[241] Aghion, Philippe; Dewatripont, Mathias; Du, Luosha; Harrison, Ann; Legros, Patrick. *Industrial Policy and Competition*, NBER Working Paper Series. https://www.nber.org/system/files/working_papers/w18048/w18048.pdf Retrieved on August 19, 2021.

[242] *Local IC policies and subsidies only gave companies "fish", but not abilities to catch "fish" by themselves*, Electric Engineering World, August 6, 2018. http://news.moore.ren/industry/21444.htm Retrieved on August 11, 2021.

[243] *Local IC policies and subsidies only gave companies "fish", but not abilities to catch "fish" by themselves*, Electric Engineering World, August 6, 2018. http://news.moore.ren/industry/21444.htm Retrieved on August 11, 2021.

[244] *Intel Reports Fourth-Quarter and Full-Year 2020 Financial Results*, Intel official website. https://www.intc.com/news-events/press-releases/detail/1439/intel-reports-fourth-quarter-and-full-year-2020-financial Retrieved on August 11, 2021.

[245] *300,000 talent shortage in the IC sector, which faces difficulty to accelerate growth*, Technology Daily, December 13, 2017. http://ip.people.com.cn/n1/2017/1213/c136680-29703648.html Retrieved on August 11, 2021.

[246] Zhou, Yixue. *Domestic semiconductor sector investment reached over RMB140 billion in 2020, a historical high*, Jiemian News, January 18, 2021. https://www.sohu.com/a/445279552_313745 Retrieved on August 11, 2021.

[247] *Sales of Logic ICs Account for Largest Share of China's IC Market in 2020*, IC Insights, February 18, 2021. https://www.icinsights.com/news/bulletins/Sales-Of-Logic-ICs-Account-For-Largest-Share-Of-Chinas-IC-Market-In-2020/ Retrieved on August 11, 2021.

[248] *AI algorithms firms pursue the chips market, but how do they break the challenges of commercialization?* China Electronics News, March 3, 2021. http://m.cena.com.cn/ai/20210303/110801.html Retrieved on August 11, 2021.

[249] Zhu, Banglin. *Harvard PhD founded a chip dream team: dedicated to build a great chip company after raising RMB1.1 billion*, Sohu.com, June 17, 2020. https://www.sohu.com/a/402512389_100008055 Retrieved on August 11, 2021.

[250] *China imports ICs worth over $100 billion each year, and these five companies are the big winners*, 36kr.com, March 29, 2018. https://www.36kr.com/p/1722392133633 Retrieved on August 12, 2021.

[251] Varas, Antonio; Varadarajan, Raj; Goodrich, Jimmy; Yinug, Falan. *Strengthening the Global Semiconductor Supply Chain in an Uncertain Era*. Boston Consulting Group, Semiconductor Industry Association, April 2021. https://www.semiconductors.org/wp-content/uploads/2021/05/BCG-x-SIA-Strengthening-the-Global-Semiconductor-Value-Chain-April-2021_1.pdf Retrieved on August 16, 2021.

[252] *Foundry downturn hits bottom, but fab utilization rates continue to fall*, EETimes, July 17, 2001. https://www.eetimes.com/foundry-downturn-hits-bottom-but-fab-utilization-rates-continue-to-fall/ Retrieved on August 10, 2021.

[253] Woo, Stu. *The U.S. Is Back in the 5G Game*, The Wall Street Journal, May 26, 2021. https://www.wsj.com/articles/us-5g-companies-11621870061 Retrieved on August 17, 2021.

[254] La Monica, Paul R. *SEC temporarily halts approvals of new Chinese IPOs after Didi debacle*, CNN.com, August 2, 2021. https://www.cnn.com/2021/07/30/investing/china-ipos-sec-freeze/index.html Retrieved on August 17, 2021.

[255] Wang, Maya. *China's Techno-Authoritarianism Has Gone Global*, Human Rights Watch, April 8, 2021. https://www.hrw.org/news/2021/04/08/chinas-techno-authoritarianism-has-gone-global Retrieved on August 18, 2021.

[256] Weiss, Jessica Chen. *Understanding and Rolling Back Digital Authoritarianism*, War On The Rocks, February 17, 2020. https://warontherocks.com/2020/02/understanding-and-rolling-back-digital-authoritarianism/ Retrieved on August 18, 2021.

[257] Zuboff, Shoshana. (2019) *The Age of Surveillance Capitalism: The Fight for a Human Future at the New Frontier of Power*. New York: PublicAffairs.

[258] Yang, Yingzhi; Goh, Brenda. *Beijing took stake and board seat in key ByteDance domestic entity this year*, Reuters, August 17, 2021. https://www.reuters.com/world/china/beijing-owns-stakes-bytedance-weibo-domestic-entities-records-show-2021-08-17/ Retrieved on August 18, 2021.

[259] Tian, Fangmeng. *The China Model and Innovation Performance—Multiple Determinants of the "Great Leap Forward" in Science and Technology*, Journal of Public Administration, Volume 6, 2017, p. 209-210.

[260] Fu, Lin. *Fudan University: initiating investigation regarding Dr. Zhang Wenhong's PhD thesis*, RFI, August 16, 2021.

https://www.rfi.fr/cn/%E4%B8%AD%E5%9B%BD/20210815-%E5%A4%8D%E6%97%A6%E5%A4%A7%E5%AD%A6-%E5%AF%B9%E5%BC%A0%E6%96%87%E5%AE%8F%E5%8D%9A%E5%A3%AB%E5%AD%A6%E4%BD%8D%E8%AE%BA%E6%96%87%E9%97%AE%E9%A2%98%E5%90%AF%E5%8A%A8%E8%B0%83%E6%9F%A5 Retrieved on August 16, 2021.

Printed in France by Amazon
Brétigny-sur-Orge, FR

16753803R00092